AI For Executives

AI Unleashed: Navigating the AI Revolution as a Business Executive

Demystifying Artificial Intelligence and Generative AI: A Practical Guide for Business Leaders

Mark Kelly

Mark Kelly 2023

AI Unleashed: Navigating the AI Revolution as a Business Executive

Demystifying Artificial Intelligence and Generative AI: A Practical Guide for Business Leaders

Mark Kelly

Amazon Press

Dublin, Ireland

Copyright 2023 AI Ireland CLG LTD

All rights reserved.

Disclaimer

The information provided in this book is intended for informational purposes only. The author and publisher disclaim any liability that may arise from the use or application of the information contained herein.

No part of this publication may be reproduced, stored in, or introduced into a retrieval system, or transmitted, in any form, or by any means (electronic, mechanical, photocopying, recording, or otherwise), without the proper permission of the publisher. Requests for permission to reproduce material from this work should be directed to AI Ireland.

The web addresses referenced in this book were live and correct at the time of the book's publication but may be subject to change.

Library of Congress Cataloguing-in-Publication Data.

Name: Mark Kelly, author

Title: AI Unleashed: Navigating the AI Revolution as a Business Executive

Description:

ISBN: 9798860550827

Subjects: Technological Innovations. / Artificial Intelligence. / Business-Data processing

CONTENTS

LEADING IN THE AI ERA. WHAT'S OUR STRATEGY? 19
    INTRODUCTION 19

CHAPTER 1:

DEMYSTIFYING ARTIFICIAL INTELLIGENCE: WHAT IS AI? 21
    KEY TAKEAWAYS 21
    INTRODUCTION 21
    AI'S SPECTRUM: UNDERSTANDING THE TYPES 22
    NARROW AI 22
    ARTIFICIAL GENERAL INTELLIGENCE (AGI) 23
        1..1. Superintelligent AI 23
    HISTORICAL EVOLUTION OF AI: FROM MYTH TO REALITY 23
    DEBUNKING AI MYTHS: SEPARATING FACT FROM FICTION 23
        1..1. AI vs Robotics 23
        1..2. Job Impact 24
        1..3. Data Dependency 24
        1..4. Author's Insight: Bridging Theory and Experience 24
    RECOMMENDATIONS 25
    CONCLUSION 26
    FOOTNOTES 26

CHAPTER 2:

HARNESSING ARTIFICIAL INTELLIGENCE FOR GOOD: A MULTI-INDUSTRY PERSPECTIVE 27
    KEY TAKEAWAYS 27
    INTRODUCTION 27
    REAL-WORLD APPLICATIONS OF AI 28
    AUTHOR'S INSIGHT: CONVERSATIONS WITH IBM WATSON HEALTH 30
    ETHICAL IMPLICATIONS 31
    MARKET TRENDS 31
    RECOMMENDATIONS 31
    CONCLUSION 32
    FOOTNOTES 32

CHAPTER 3:
THE ROLE OF DATA FOR AI AT THE EXECUTIVE LEVEL 34
- Key Takeaways 34
- Introduction 34
- Author's Insight 34
- Predictive Intelligence and Its Significance 35
- Challenges in Harnessing Data 35
- Data Governance and Ethical Concerns 35
- Data Strategy: The Bedrock of AI 36
- Recommendations 37
- Leadership in the Age of Data and AI 37
- Trends in Data and AI Leadership 37
- Future Trends in Data and AI 38
- Conclusion 38
- Footnotes 38

CHAPTER 4:
THE INDISPENSABLE ROLE OF DATA LITERACY 39
- Key Takeaways 40
- Introduction 40
- The Training Gap 40
- Data Storytelling and Real-World Applications 41
- The Multiple Facets of Data 41
- Role of Data in AI 41
- AI Ethics and Social Responsibility 41
- The Intricate Process of Model Training 42
- Challenges and Considerations 42
- The Role of Interdisciplinary Teams 42
- Leadership's Role in AI Adoption 43
- Creating an AI-Ready Culture 43
- Author's Insight: The Human Factor in AI 43
- Recommendations: 43
- Conclusion 44
- Footnotes 44

PART 2
CHAPTER 5:
RETURN ON INVESTMENT (ROI) FROM AI 45
- KEY TAKEAWAYS 45
- INTRODUCTION 45
- SECTION 1: CHALLENGES OF AI IMPLEMENTATION IN ENTERPRISES. 45
- SECTION 2: CAUSES OF THESE CHALLENGES. 47
- SECTION 3: CALCULATING ROI FROM AI PROJECTS. 48
- AUTHOR'S INSIGHT: THE ROI PARADOX IN AI 49
- RECOMMENDATIONS 49
- CONCLUSION 50
- FOOTNOTES 51

CHAPTER 6:
AI AND CUSTOMER EXPERIENCE 52
- KEY TAKEAWAYS 52
- INTRODUCTION 53
- SECTION 1: THE POTENTIAL AND RISKS OF AI 54
  - 6..1. The Promise of AI 54
  - 6..2. The Risk of Misplaced Priorities 54
- SECTION 2: THE CENTRALITY OF CUSTOMER LOVE 54
  - 6..1. Every Interaction Matters 54
  - 6..2. Enriching Customers' Lives 55
- SECTION 3: PERSONALIZING THE CUSTOMER EXPERIENCE 55
  - 6..1. Rethinking Objective Functions 55
  - 6..2. The Power of Personalization 56
- AUTHOR'S INSIGHT 56
- CASE STUDY 1: LEVERAGING AI TO MONITOR CUSTOMER SENTIMENT ON SOCIAL MEDIA 56
- CASE STUDY 2: DOMINO'S PIZZA AND THE AI-DRIVEN CUSTOMER SERVICE 57
- RECOMMENDATIONS 58
- CONCLUSION 58
- FOOTNOTES 59

CHAPTER 7:
IN-DEPTH LOOK AT GENERATIVE AI FOR BUSINESS 60
- KEY TAKEAWAYS 60
- INTRODUCTION TO GENERATIVE AI 60
- EVALUATING GENERATIVE AI MODEL 61
- REAL-WORLD APPLICATIONS OF GENERATIVE AI 61

LIMITATIONS OF GENERATIVE AI 64
GENERATIVE AI IN BUSINESS: INSIGHTS FROM KPMG SURVEY AUGUST 2023 64
RECOMMENDATIONS FOR OVERCOMING LIMITATIONS: 65
RECOMMENDATIONS FOR IMPLEMENTING GENERATIVE AI: 65
IMPACT ON THE WORKFORCE 66
AUTHOR'S INSIGHT AND SUMMARY 66
CONCLUSION 67
FOOTNOTES 67

CHAPTER 8:

AI IN MARKETING AND SALES 69

KEY TAKEAWAYS 69
INTRODUCTION 69
THE STRATEGIC IMPERATIVE OF AI IN MARKETING AND SALES 69
CASE STUDIES: REAL-WORLD APPLICATIONS 70
   8..1. Nutella: Personalized Marketing Campaigns 70
   8..2. Volkswagen: AI-Driven Ad Buying 70
   8..3. Strategic Alignment: The Key to AI Success in Marketing and Sales . 71
   8..4. AI-Enabled Marketing: Personalization at Its Best 71
   8..5. AI in Sales: Enhancing Customer Engagement and Efficiency 71
AUTHOR'S INSIGHTS 71
RECOMMENDATIONS 72
ETHICAL AND PRIVACY CONSIDERATIONS IN AI ADOPTION 72
   8..1. Data Privacy 72
   8..2. Algorithmic Bias 73
   8..3. Transparency 73
   8..4. Consumer Consent 73
CONCLUSION: STRIKING THE RIGHT BALANCE 73
FOOTNOTES 74

CHAPTER 9:

PINPOINTING AI OPPORTUNITIES WITHIN YOUR BUSINESS 75

KEY TAKEAWAYS: 75
INTRODUCTION 75
IDENTIFYING AI OPPORTUNITIES IN YOUR BUSINESS 75
ALIGNING AI INITIATIVES WITH BUSINESS GOALS 76
MANAGING AI PROJECTS 76
MONITORING AND EVALUATING AI PROJECT SUCCESS 76
CHECKLIST FOR PINPOINTING AI OPPORTUNITIES 77
AUTHOR'S INSIGHTS 77
RECOMMENDATIONS 78

CONCLUSION 78

CHAPTER 10:

LEVERAGING AI IN SMALL AND MEDIUM BUSINESSES (SMBS): DRIVING GROWTH AND INNOVATION 79

KEY TAKEAWAYS 79
INTRODUCTION 79
SECTION 1: THE CURRENT STATE OF AI IN SMBS 80
SECTION 2: THE BENEFITS OF AI FOR SMBS.. 80
    10..1.   *Subsection 2.1: Streamlining and Automating Processes.............. 81*
    10..2.   *Subsection 2.2: Enhancing Productivity and Innovation 81*
    10..3.   *Subsection 2.3: Improving Work Quality and Saving Time........... 81*
SECTION 3: CHALLENGES OF IMPLEMENTING AI IN SMBS................................... 82
    10..1.   *Subsection 3.1: Lack of Resources 82*
    10..2.   *Subsection 3.2: Data Privacy and Security Concerns 82*
    10..3.   *Subsection 3.3: Skills Gap and Learning Curve............................ 82*
SECTION 4: AI APPLICATIONS FOR SMBS 83
    10..1.   *Subsection 4.1: Customer Service Automation.............................. 83*
    10..2.   *Subsection 4.2: Personalized Marketing 83*
    10..3.   *Subsection 4.3: E-commerce and Inventory Management.............. 84*
    SECTION 5: PRACTICAL AI APPLICATIONS IN SPECIFIC SMALL BUSINESS SCENARIOS... 84
    10..1.   *Subsection 5.1: Inventory Management for a Family-Owned Takeaway Outlet 84*
    10..2.   *Subsection 5.2: Stock Management for a T-Shirt Shop Using Computer Vision 85*
AUTHOR'S INSIGHTS 85
RECOMMENDATIONS 86
    CHECKLIST FOR PINPOINTING AI OPPORTUNITIES WITHIN YOUR BUSINESS (APPENDIX)... 86
CONCLUSION 87
FOOTNOTES 87

PART 3

AI CONCEPTS AND MANAGEMENT

CHAPTER 11:

THE POWER OF EXPLAINABLE AI (XAI) 88

- KEY TAKEAWAYS: 88
- INTRODUCTION: THE IMPERATIVE OF TRANSPARENCY 88
- THE ESSENCE OF EXPLAINABLE AI 89
- THE BROAD SPECTRUM OF XAI APPLICATIONS 89
- PILLARS OF XAI 90
- TOOLS AND TECHNIQUES 90
- CHALLENGES ON THE HORIZON 91
- EXPERT INSIGHTS 92
- THE FUTURE LANDSCAPE OF XAI 92
- AUTHOR'S PERSONAL INSIGHTS 92
- RECOMMENDATIONS 93
- CASE STUDY: XAI IN HEALTHCARE 93
- CONCLUSION: CHARTING A TRANSPARENT PATH FORWARD 93

CHAPTER 12: 95

DISPELLING AI FEARS: A DATA-BACKED PERSPECTIVE 95

- KEY TAKEAWAYS 95
- INTRODUCTION DISPELLING AI FEARS THROUGH TRANSPARENCY 95
- UNRAVELLING THE JOB LOSS MYTH 96
- THE DAWN OF NEW PROFESSIONS 96
- AI AS A COLLABORATOR, NOT COMPETITOR 96
- AUTHOR'S INSIGHTS 97
- RECOMMENDATIONS FOR THE READER 97
- CONCLUSION 98
- FOOTNOTES 98

CHAPTER 13:

RECOGNIZING THE NEED FOR EXTERNAL AI EXPERTISE 100

- INTRODUCTION: AI - A COLLABORATIVE ENDEAVOR 100
- SECTION 1: WHEN TO SEEK EXTERNAL AI EXPERTISE 100
- SECTION 2: IDENTIFYING THE IDEAL AI PARTNER 101
- SECTION 3: CULTIVATING A PRODUCTIVE AI PARTNERSHIP 102
- SECTION 4: ASSESSING POTENTIAL AI VENDORS 102
    - CASE STUDY: TRANSFORMING VENDOR INTERACTION THROUGH CONSULTANCY EXPERTISE 103

AUTHOR'S INSIGHTS 104
RECOMMENDATIONS 105
CONCLUSION 105
FOOTNOTES 105

CHAPTER 14:

AI IN PROJECT MANAGEMENT - UNLEASHING THE POWER OF AI .. 106

KEY TAKEAWAYS 106
INTRODUCTION 106
THE AI-POWERED EVOLUTION OF PROJECT MANAGEMENT: 106
STREAMLINING ADMINISTRATIVE EFFICIENCY: 107
RESHAPING PROJECT SCOPE AND LEADERSHIP WITH AI: 107
AI IN ACTION: REAL-WORLD USE CASES: 107
SWIFT AND EFFICIENT INTEGRATION: 108
  INSIGHTS FROM THE "UNLEASHING THE POWER OF ARTIFICIAL INTELLIGENCE IN
  PROJECT MANAGEMENT" SURVEY: 109
AUTHOR'S INSIGHTS 109
RECOMMENDATIONS 110
FUTURE OUTLOOK 110
CONCLUSION 110
FOOTNOTES 111

CHAPTER 15

OVERCOMING AI PROJECT FAILURES: RISKS AND REMEDIES 113

KEY TAKEAWAYS 113
INTRODUCTION 113
THE REALITY OF AI PROJECT FAILURES 114
ORGANIZATIONAL AND TECHNOLOGICAL CHALLENGES 114
UNEARTHING THE CRITICAL FACTORS 115
EMPIRICAL INSIGHTS: UNDERSTANDING THE CRITICAL FACTORS 116
LESSONS FROM THE PANDEMIC: WHERE AI FELL SHORT 116
MOVING FORWARD: REMEDIES AND BEST PRACTICES 117
THE ROLE OF CULTURE IN AI PROJECT FAILURES 118
AUTHOR'S INSIGHTS 119
CASE STUDIES 119
FUTURE OUTLOOK 120
CONCLUSION 120
FOOTNOTES 121

CHAPTER 16:
MASTERING AI SKILLS AND TALENT ACQUISITION 122

- KEY TAKEAWAYS: 122
- INTRODUCTION 122
- SECTION 1: NAVIGATING THE AI REVOLUTION 123
  - 16..1. Riding the AI Wave 123
- SECTION 2: BUILDING AN AI-SAVVY TEAM 123
  - 16..1. Attracting New Talent 123
  - 16..2. Continuous Training and Development 124
- SECTION 3: THE AI SKILLSET 124
  - 16..1. Technical Skills 124
  - 16..2. Business Skills 125
  - 16..3. Ethical and Legal Skills 125
- SECTION 4: THE ROLE OF LEADERSHIP 126
  - 16..1. Cultivating a Learning Culture 126
  - 16..2. Leading by Example 126
- AUTHOR'S INSIGHTS 126
- RECOMMENDATIONS 127
- CONCLUSION 127
- FOOTNOTES 128

PART IV
ETHICAL AND REGULATORY CONSIDERATIONS
CHAPTER 17:
THE ETHICAL DIMENSION: KEY CONSIDERATIONS IN AI DEPLOYMENT 129

- KEY TAKEAWAYS 129
- INTRODUCTION 129
- SECTION 1: UNLOCKING AI'S POTENTIAL 130
  - 17..1. 1.1 Guide to Identifying AI Opportunities: 130
- SECTION 2: THE ETHICAL COMPASS OF AI 131
  - 17..1. Ethical Considerations Checklist for Business Leaders: 131
- SECTION 3: PREPARING FOR THE FUTURE OF AI 132
  - 17..1. Continuous Learning for Business-wide concern. 132
  - 17..2. Cross-Functional Collaboration 132
  - 17..3. Ethical Leadership for Long-Term Success 132
  - 17..4. Staying Ahead of the Regulatory Curve 133
  - 17..5. Understanding AI's Broader Impact 133
- SECTION 4: CASE STUDY 133

    17..1.   Case Study: Navigating Ethical Complexities in AI-Driven Healthcare *133*
    SECTION 5: THE ROLE OF LEADERSHIP IN AI INTEGRATION 134
        17..1.   Fostering a Learning Culture *134*
        17..2.   Leading Through Action *134*
        17..3.   Ethical Governance *134*
        17..4.   Strategic Foresight *134*
    RECOMMENDATIONS 135
        17..1.   Ethical Oversight *135*
        17..2.   Data Governance *135*
        17..3.   Skill Development Initiatives *135*
        17..4.   Stakeholder Involvement *135*
        17..5.   Transparency and Accountability *136*
        17..6.   Legal Readiness *136*
        17..7.   Author's Insights *136*
    CONCLUSION 137
    FOOTNOTES 138

CHAPTER 18:
AI GOVERNANCE AND ETHICS 139

    KEY TAKEAWAYS 139
    INTRODUCTION 139
    DATA GOVERNANCE: THE LIFEBLOOD OF AI 139
    AI MODEL MANAGEMENT: THE EVOLUTION OF AI 140
    OVERSIGHT MECHANISMS: GUIDING THE AI JOURNEY 140
    AUTHOR'S INSIGHTS 140
    DATA GOVERNANCE: THE FOUNDATION FOR ETHICAL AI 141
    KEY RECOMMENDATIONS FOR DATA GOVERNANCE 141
    AI MODEL MANAGEMENT: NAVIGATING THE AI LIFECYCLE 141
    KEY RECOMMENDATIONS FOR AI MODEL MANAGEMENT 141
    UNIFIED GUIDELINES FOR ETHICAL AND COMPLIANT AI GOVERNANCE 142
    CONCLUSION 143
    FOOTNOTES 144

CHAPTER 19:
THE AI ACT AND EU PROPOSED REGULATION WITH A COMPARATIVE LOOK AT U.S. DEVELOPMENTS 145

    KEY TAKEAWAYS 145
    INTRODUCTION 146
    THE AI ACT 146
    ETHICAL CONSIDERATIONS 147

BUSINESSES RESERVATIONS AND CONCERNS OF REGULATION 147
    19..1.   *Technological Sovereignty*... *147*
GLOBAL REGULATORY LANDSCAPE IN AI 148
U.S. DEVELOPMENTS IN AI REGULATION 148
    19..1.   *Voluntary Safeguards* *148*
        19..1.1.   Legislative Landscape 148
EXECUTIVE ORDER 149
INTERNATIONAL COLLABORATION 149
THE EUROPEAN UNION'S REGULATORY FRAMEWORK FOR AI 149
RECOMMENDATIONS 151
AUTHOR'S INSIGHTS: NAVIGATING THE REGULATORY LANDSCAPE OF AI 153
CONCLUSION 153
FOOTNOTES 154

CHAPTER 20:

UNMASKING THE HIDDEN COSTS OF AI – LIABILITY, RISKS, AND FINANCIAL CONSIDERATIONS 155

KEY TAKEAWAYS 155
INTRODUCTION 155
SECTION 1: FINANCIAL ASPECTS OF AI INTEGRATION 156
    20..1.   *The Financial Commitment of Integrating AI into Business Operations*.. *156*
    20..2.   *Case Study: IBM's AI Adoption* *157*
    20..3.   *Operational Expenses: The Costs You Didn't See Coming*........... *158*
ROI REALITIES: BALANCING COSTS AND BENEFITS 158
SECTION 2: OPERATIONAL ADJUSTMENTS... 159
    20..1.   *Operational Adjustments: The Need for Organisational Changes 159*
SECTION 3: HIDDEN COSTS 159
    20..1.   *Hidden Costs: The Expenses You Didn't Anticipate* *159*
SECTION 4: LEGAL COMPLEXITIES 160
    20..1.   *Liability Challenges: Navigating the Legal Maze* *160*
    20..2.   *Future Legal Landscape: Staying Ahead of the Curve* *160*
SECTION 5: RISK MANAGEMENT 161
    20..1.   *AI Insurance: Safeguarding Your Investment*............................... *161*
    20..2.   *Risk Assessment Tools: Quantifying the Unknown* *161*
SECTION 6: ETHICAL CONCERNS: THE REPUTATIONAL ASPECT......................... 161
    20..1.   *Ethical Concerns: Balancing Innovation and Responsibility* *161*
    20..2.   *Sustainable AI: The Green Side of Intelligence* *162*
AUTHOR'S INSIGHTS 162
RECOMMENDATIONS 163
CONCLUSION 163

FOOTNOTES 164

CHAPTER 21:
ETHICAL AND ECONOMIC IMPLICATIONS OF AI IN CYBERSECURITY
.... 166

    KEY TAKEAWAYS 166
    INTRODUCTION 166
    THE ECONOMIC IMPERATIVE OF AI IN CYBERSECURITY 167
    CASE STUDIES: REAL-WORLD APPLICATIONS AND LESSONS LEARNED 167
    FUTURE TRENDS: THE EVOLVING LANDSCAPE OF AI AND CYBERSECURITY 168
    AUTHOR'S INSIGHTS: NAVIGATING THE FUTURE OF AI IN CYBERSECURITY 169
    RECOMMENDATIONS 170
    CONCLUSION 170
    FOOTNOTES 171

CHAPTER 22:
CASE STUDIES OF SUCCESSFUL AI IMPLEMENTATION 172

    INTRODUCTION 172
    1.1 DIAGNOSTICS 173
    1.2 ADMINISTRATIVE EFFICIENCY 174
    2.1 FRAUD DETECTION 174
    2.2 INVESTMENT MANAGEMENT 174
    3.1 EMPLOYEE RECOGNITION AND PERFORMANCE 175
    3.2 RECRUITMENT 175
    4.1 CUSTOMER ENGAGEMENT 175
    4.2 CAMPAIGN OPTIMISATION 175
    AUTHOR'S INSIGHT 176
    RECOMMENDATIONS FOR BUSINESSES 177
    ETHICAL AI USE 177
    EMPLOYEE UPSKILLING 177
    COLLABORATION WITH ACADEMIA 177
    CUSTOMER-FIRST APPROACH 177
    CONCLUSION 179
    FOOTNOTES 180

CHAPTER 23:
THE FUTURE OF WORK WITH AI 181

    KEY TAKEAWAYS 181
    INTRODUCTION: THE AI REVOLUTION BEGINS 181
    AI AS A COLLABORATIVE PARTNER IN THE WORKPLACE 182

Navigating the AI Landscape: A Comprehensive Dive into the Future of Work 182
The Role Reversal 182
Expanding Ideas and Solutions 183
AI's Revolutionary Impact 183
AI's Expansive Reach 183
AI as a Sounding Board 183
Efficiency in White-Collar Jobs 184
The GenAI Adaptation 184
Ethical Implications of AI in the Workplace 184
Increasing Accuracy and Addressing Biases 185
Training, Reskilling, and the Global Perspective 185
McKinsey's Insights: The Changing American Work Landscape 185
The Future Job Landscape 185
Author's Insights 186
Challenges, Limitations, and the Road Ahead 186
Recommendations 186
Conclusion: Charting the AI Era 187
Footnotes 188

CHAPTER 24:

NAVIGATING THE GLOBAL AI LANDSCAPE FOR EXECUTIVES 189

Key Takeaways 189
Introduction 189
The Major Players in AI 190
Emerging Markets in AI 190
Regulatory Environment 191
Market Dynamics 192
Cultural Nuances 192
Technological Infrastructure 193
Challenges in Achieving AI Leadership 193
Strategies for Fostering AI Development 194
Author's Insights 194
Ensuring Strategic Competitiveness in AI 194
The Future of the Global AI Landscape 195
Recommendations for Executives 195
Conclusion 195
Footnotes 197

CHAPTER 25:

EXPLORING EMERGING AI TRENDS AND TECHNOLOGIES: NAVIGATING THE FUTURE OF BUSINESS 198

    KEY TAKEAWAYS 198
    INTRODUCTION 198
    TOP TRENDS IN EDGE COMPUTING 199
        25..1.   *Prioritising Security and Privacy* *199*
        25..2.   *The Importance of Edge-to-Cloud Interoperability* *199*
        25..3.   *The Role of Edge AI and Machine Learning* *199*
        25..4.   *The Impact of 5G Adoption* *199*
        25..5.   *The Emergence of Edge-as-a-Service (EaaS)* *200*
        25..6.   *Quantum Computing* *201*
        25..7.   *Autonomous Vehicles* *201*
        25..8.   *The Metaverse* *201*
        25..9.   *AI and Climate Change Mitigation* *201*
    AUTHOR'S INSIGHTS: NAVIGATING THE FUTURE THROUGH EMERGING AI TRENDS 201
    RECOMMENDATIONS: 203
    CONCLUSION 203
    FOOTNOTES 203

CHAPTER 26:

EMBRACING AI: A STRATEGIC BLUEPRINT FOR TOMORROW'S LEADERS 204

    KEY TAKEAWAYS 204
    INTRODUCTION 204
    UNDERSTANDING AI 205
    REAL-WORLD USES OF AI 205
    ETHICS AND AI 205
    DATA'S ROLE IN AI 205
    NAVIGATING THE AI MATURITY LADDER 206
    COLLABORATION: THE KEY TO AI INNOVATION 206
    THE HORIZON OF AI 207
    MANAGING CHANGE IN THE AI ERA 207
    AI AND LEADERSHIP 207
    AI AND STRATEGY 207
    METRICS AND KPIS: EVALUATING AI SUCCESS 207
    AI AND TALENT 208
    CUSTOMER ENGAGEMENT METRICS 208
    COST SAVINGS 208
    TIME-TO-VALUE 208

ETHICAL AND FAIRNESS METRICS 208
AI AND TALENT 209
AI AND CUSTOMERS 209
AUTHOR'S INSIGHTS 209
RECOMMENDATIONS 209
ACTIONABLE STEPS FOR LEADERS: IMPLEMENTING AI IN YOUR ORGANIZATION 210
CONCLUSION 212
FOOTNOTES 213

CHAPTER 27:

CONCLUSION AND FINAL THOUGHTS: AI FOR EXECUTIVES 214

INTRODUCTION 214
TRANSFORMING WORK WITH AI 214
ETHICAL CONSIDERATIONS 214
LEARNING FROM OTHERS 215
STAYING AHEAD WITH AI 215
A CALL TO ACTION FOR LEADERS 215
CONCLUSION 216

28. POSTSCRIPT FROM THE AUTHOR 217

Table of Figures

FIGURE 1.1 22

FIGURE 2.1 30

FIGURE 3.1 36

FIGURE 4.1 39

FIGURE 6.1 53

FIGURE 19.1 150

FIGURE 22.1 173

Innovation distinguishes between a leader and a follower.

– Steve Jobs

Leading in the AI Era. What's Our Strategy?

Introduction

Curious about how AI is changing our world? How it's making businesses smarter and opening new doors? If you're a business leader trying to understand all this "AI stuff", this book is perfect for you.

AI is a big deal these days. It's changing how companies work and bringing up opportunities we didn't think were possible before. I got into AI by chance in 2018 when I had a chat with an expert in a Dublin café. That chat led me to meet over 450 AI experts from big companies like Google and Microsoft to small start-ups.

I've learned a lot from these experts, and I've put all that knowledge into this book. I run AI Ireland, where we always talk about AI and share what we know. This book is all about helping business leaders understand AI and use it in their companies.

"AI Unleashed: Navigating the AI Revolution as a Business Executive" is more than just facts. It's a guide. It'll help you understand AI and how it's changing business. We'll talk about the real stuff, like how to use AI in your company and the challenges you might face.

AI is doing some cool things. It's not just about automating tasks anymore. It's about humans and machines working together in new ways. Think about factories where robots work alongside people or new robots being made by companies like Fourier and Tesla.

AI is everywhere. For example, Coca Cola recently used AI in an advertisement and plans to use it to improve customer experiences. With AI, businesses can quickly analyse lots of data, helping them make better decisions and save money.

From sales to customer service, AI is making a difference. By the end of this book, you'll understand AI and be ready to use it in your business.

Come along, and let's explore AI together.

1. Chapter 1:

Demystifying Artificial Intelligence: What is AI?

Key Takeaways

1. AI operates across a spectrum, from Narrow AI to Superintelligent AI.

2. Understanding AI requires a look into its historical evolution and its future potential.

3. Debunking common AI myths helps create a more informed perspective.

Introduction

Artificial Intelligence (AI) is not just a term for the technologically inclined; it's a transformative force across industries and societies. This chapter aims to unravel the intricate threads that make up AI, from its historical roots to its modern applications and beyond. The AI Industry is currently valued at $207.9 billion in 2023 and is expected to increase dramatically by 788.64% to reach an unprecedented $1.87 trillion by 2030. This remarkable growth trajectory is projected to exceed the $1 trillion benchmark in 2028. Consensus predictions are centred around robust growth in the AI market over the next decade[1].

AI's Spectrum: Understanding the Types

There are three primary categories of AI, as depicted in Figure 1.1 AI's Spectrum: Understanding the Types. Figure 1.1

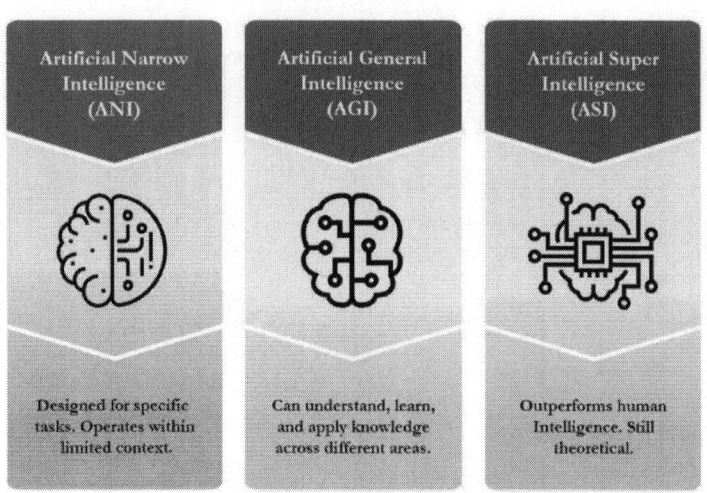

Figure 1.1

Narrow AI

Narrow AI, commonly referred to as Weak AI, is specialized in performing a singular task. These systems lack the capabilities for consciousness, emotions, or generalized intelligence. Notable examples encompass search algorithms and image recognition software. The utility of Narrow AI is expanding, particularly in the realm of data-driven business operations.

Artificial General Intelligence (AGI)

AGI aims to emulate human-like cognitive functions, enabling the system to learn and apply knowledge across diverse domains. While AGI remains an aspirational objective, its eventual realization would signify a transformative advancement, ushering us into an epoch where machines could undertake any intellectual endeavour achievable by humans.

1..1. Superintelligent AI

Superintelligent AI is a theoretical construct that posits a form of AI surpassing human intelligence across virtually all disciplines. This notion is both exhilarating and contentious, eliciting ethical and safety deliberations among academics and ethicists alike.

Historical Evolution of AI: From Myth to Reality

The history of AI dates back far beyond modern computing. Stories and myths about beings endowed with intelligence can be found in ancient cultures. Fast forward to the 20th century, and pioneers like Alan Turing[1] and John McCarthy[2] have laid the foundational theories that led to the AI of today.

Debunking AI Myths: Separating Fact from Fiction

1..1. AI vs Robotics

Contrary to popular belief, AI and robotics are not synonymous. Robots can be programmed without using AI, and AI systems don't require a physical body to function.

1..2. Job Impact

A prevalent misconception is that AI will result in substantial unemployment. In reality, AI often generates more job opportunities than it eradicates by automating routine tasks, thereby enabling humans to focus on more intricate duties. However, it's crucial to delve into the complexities of this issue, as certain roles are indeed being supplanted. Additionally, it's noteworthy that as employees depart due to natural attrition, they are not invariably replaced by human counterparts, but increasingly by AI systems.

1..3. Data Dependency

AI systems are only as good as the data they are trained on. Biased or flawed data can lead to inaccurate or unjust decisions, reinforcing the importance of quality data.

1..4. Author's Insight: Bridging Theory and Experience

In my extensive dialogues with AI industry leaders, the transformative potential of AI emerges as a consistent theme. While there's palpable excitement about AI's capabilities, there's also caution regarding its limitations and ethical implications. The earlier iterations of AI have been quietly powering various sectors for years, often unnoticed. Whether it's the recommendation algorithms on Netflix or the automation in medical diagnostics, this "background AI" has been subtly shaping our experiences.

However, the landscape is rapidly evolving. The advent of generative AI technologies like OpenAI's ChatGPT marks a shift from this background role to a more conspicuous, front-and-center presence. This latest surge in AI is not merely faster; it is also more accessible and conspicuous, taking many by surprise.

As we delve deeper into the subsequent chapters of this book, we will explore the multifaceted impact of AI on business. We'll examine how AI is revolutionizing customer service, transforming healthcare, and even reshaping the way we think about ethics and governance. This shift underscores the need for a nuanced understanding of AI's role across different sectors. It's no longer just a tool working in the background; it's becoming an integral part of our daily interactions and decision-making processes.

By bridging theory and real-world applications, this book aims to provide a comprehensive view of the transformative power and challenges of AI in the modern business landscape.

Recommendations

1. **Stay Informed:** Regularly update your knowledge on AI advancements.

2. **Data Quality:** Invest in collecting and maintaining high-quality data.

3. **Ethical Practices:** Prioritize ethics in AI application and management.

Conclusion

Understanding AI is crucial for modern executives. By debunking myths, grasping its history, and understanding its types, one can better appreciate its transformative impact. As we transition into subsequent chapters, the focus will shift to applying this foundational knowledge across various business functions.

Footnotes

1. AI Could Become A Trillion Dollar Industry In The Next 5 Years

https://finance.yahoo.com/news/ai-could-become-trillion-dollar-130000958.html?guccounter=1&guce_referrer=aHR0cHM6Ly93d3cuZ29vZ2xlLmNvbS8&guce_referrer_sig=AQAAAL0T3rpSut5IVMBciWTHLsD7YMTiL8YPqXxwaGpkcRZipmHF4J3LAJGzUAwiT1_i89GoqS7LfgRVkYaGMIpmqGklYf36S0LyTzWx2Q3sMYteDeM3HZRnjxF2ivj1AgI2lpGajGqmlUzPWpCaU2qo4j8iBhbs8IubkySFqQiOJbjn

2. "Alan Turing"
https://en.wikipedia.org/wiki/Alan_Turing

3. "John McCarthy"
https://en.wikipedia.org/wiki/John_McCarthy_(computer_scientist)

2. Chapter 2:

Harnessing Artificial Intelligence for Good: A Multi-Industry Perspective

Key Takeaways

1. Realize the multi-faceted applications of AI across healthcare, manufacturing, finance, agriculture, education, retail, energy, and logistics.

2. Comprehend the financial and ethical implications of integrating AI into various industries.

3. Recognize the significance of responsible AI application for sustainable growth and societal impact.

Introduction

Artificial Intelligence has not just been a technological advancement; it's been a transformative power across various sectors. However, as we implement AI more comprehensively, the focus on ethical considerations and responsible application can't be overstated[1]. AI is already part of our daily lives, from voice assistants in our homes to autonomous vehicles on our streets. It's vital to explore how AI can be harnessed for societal benefits responsibly.

Real-world Applications of AI

Healthcare: AI has streamlined medical diagnostics and drug discovery. IBM's Watson and Google's LYNA are pivotal in personalized healthcare These technologies are not only making diagnostics more accurate but also democratizing healthcare by making it more accessible.

Manufacturing: Companies like General Electric are using AI for predictive maintenance to boost efficiency [2]. GE's Predix platform can foresee equipment failures and downtime, saving costs and time.

Finance: Financial organizations utilize AI for fraud detection and customer service automation. Generative AI can boost front-office productivity by up to 35%, leading to additional revenue of US $3.5 million[3].

Agriculture: AI algorithms are helping farmers make better decisions, leading to more sustainable farming practices[4]. Advanced predictive models analyse weather patterns and soil conditions to optimize planting schedules. Additionally, machine learning algorithms process real-time data from IoT sensors to monitor crop health, enabling timely interventions that reduce waste and increase yield[4].

Retail: AI is being utilised to personalise customer experiences and improve supply chain management. Machine learning algorithms analyse customer behaviour and preferences to curate personalized product recommendations, enhancing customer engagement and sales. On the supply chain front, AI-powered analytics tools assess real-time inventory levels and demand forecasts, enabling more efficient stock replenishment and reducing operational costs.

Energy: AI algorithms are optimizing energy production and consumption, aiding the transition to renewable resources[5]. Predictive analytics powered by AI assess weather patterns to optimize the timing and amount of renewable energy production, such as solar and wind power. Additionally, AI-driven smart grids dynamically adjust energy distribution based on real-time demand, reducing waste and enhancing sustainability.

Logistics: AI is transforming how goods are transported, reducing costs and environmental impact. Route optimization algorithms analyse traffic and road conditions in real-time, enabling more efficient fuel usage and shorter delivery times.

Figure 2.1 How AI is Applied to industry

Author's Insight: Conversations with IBM Watson Health

My journey through the world of AI has allowed me to witness first-hand the transformative power of technology. I recall a conversation with a leader from IBM Watson Health. We delved into how AI algorithms are revolutionizing cancer treatment, truly exemplifying the union of technology and compassion[5].

Ethical Implications

As AI becomes increasingly woven into the societal landscape, ethical considerations such as privacy, data security, and algorithmic fairness become paramount. If misused, AI has the potential to serve as an instrument for widespread surveillance or manipulation. Therefore, robust ethical frameworks are essential. In this book, the significance of ethical considerations in AI deployment is explored, with a focus on Explainable AI in Part III and a deep dive into Ethical and Regulatory Concerns in Part IV.

Market Trends

The AI market is poised for substantial growth, with projections indicating a surge in market value across various sectors. Specifically, the healthcare sector is anticipated to surpass a $20 billion valuation by 2023[6]. Notably, Deutsche Bank has collaborated with NVIDIA to integrate AI into the financial services industry, as evidenced by a survey involving close to 500 financial professionals globally.

Recommendations

1. Executives should prioritize investments in AI research to keep up with the rapid advancements in technology.

2. Organizations must invest in workforce training programs to bridge the skills gap in AI applications.

3. Industries should engage with policymakers to establish a framework

Conclusion

Artificial Intelligence is increasingly becoming a cornerstone in multiple sectors. From streamlining manufacturing to enhancing healthcare, the applications are virtually limitless. However, it is imperative for us to implement AI responsibly to ensure its benefits are widespread and ethical. As we delve deeper into the intricate maze of AI applications in our subsequent chapter on "The Role of Data in AI for Executives," we'll further explore how data is the lifeblood that makes all these advancements possible.

Footnotes

1. Expert Analysis & Ethical Considerations in AI – Linkedin article
https://www.linkedin.com/pulse/expert-analysis-ethical-considerations-challenges-ai-future-phillips#:~:text=Only%20by%20taking%20a%20comprehensive,the%20use%20of%20this%20technology.

2. General Electric (GE): Predictive Maintenance with AI
https://aithority.com/machine-learning/ai-and-data-science-in-action-the-top-5-ai-data-science-projects-for-manufacturing/#:~:text=General%20Electric%20(GE)%3A%20Predictive,failures%20and%20optimize%20maintenance%20schedules.

3. Deloitte Survey 2019 Art and Finance report 2019
https://www2.deloitte.com/content/dam/Deloitte/at/Documents/presse/lu-art-and-finance-report-2019.pdf

4. How data and artificial intelligence can drive Asia's sustainable farming future
https://www.weforum.org/agenda/2023/05/artificial-intelligence-sustainable-farming-asia/

5.. " AI Ireland Founder Interviews "
https://www.aiireland-awards.com/interviews

6..AI in healthcare market size worldwide from 2021 to 2030"
https://www.statista.com/statistics/1334826/ai-in-healthcare-market-size-worldwide/

3. Chapter 3:

The Role of Data for AI at the Executive Level

Key Takeaways

1. Understand the pivotal role of data in AI, forming the foundation for decision-making and fuelling AI algorithms.

2. Learn about the significance of data strategy, governance, privacy, quality, and security in the context of AI.

3. Gain insights into the current trends in global data and AI initiatives.

Introduction

Data is the lifeblood of Artificial Intelligence (AI), powering algorithms, providing insights, and forming the foundation for decision-making. As an executive, comprehending the role of data in AI is crucial as you guide AI implementation within your organization. This chapter delves into the significance of data strategy, governance, privacy, quality, and security in the context of AI.

Author's Insight

During one of my interviews with a senior executive at a multinational corporation in Ireland, it became vividly clear how impactful a data-driven approach can be. The company had faced declining sales and market share for several quarters. However, by leveraging data analytics and machine learning algorithms, they identified patterns that were previously elusive. Subtle shifts in consumer behaviour and market dynamics were unearthed, and the company adjusted its strategy accordingly. Within a year, they reversed the trend and regained market share. This experience was a powerful testament to the role of data in modern executive decision-making[1].

Predictive Intelligence and Its Significance

The evolution of AI has ushered in an era of predictive intelligence. This capability allows businesses to anticipate potential scenarios or options, determining the value of future outcomes based on past momentum and current market signals. Predictive intelligence has applications beyond merely forecasting business trends; it can help in resource allocation, supply chain optimization, and customer segmentation, among other areas.

Challenges in Harnessing Data

Despite the potential of data and AI, many businesses worldwide face challenges in Harnessing their full power. One of the primary barriers is cultural. Many organizations lack a culture that genuinely values data-driven decision-making. Other barriers include inadequate data quality, privacy concerns, and the lack of appropriate talent to make sense of large data sets.

Data Governance and Ethical Concerns

Data governance, which encompasses data security, quality, and privacy, is another critical aspect executives should focus on. Governing data isn't just about compliance with laws like GDPR; it's also about maintaining customer trust and ethical considerations. Ethical data use can provide a competitive edge and safeguard the organization against reputational risks. Later in the book we will go into the topics in more detail.

Data Strategy: The Bedrock of AI

A robust data strategy is pivotal for successful AI implementation. It aligns with business objectives and caters to the specific needs of AI systems. Building a data strategy involves identifying data types, sources, collection methods, and storage. It also includes determining how to analyse and utilize data to drive decisions. The strategy should also have a framework for evaluating the return on investment (ROI) for data and AI projects, aligning them with the business goals.

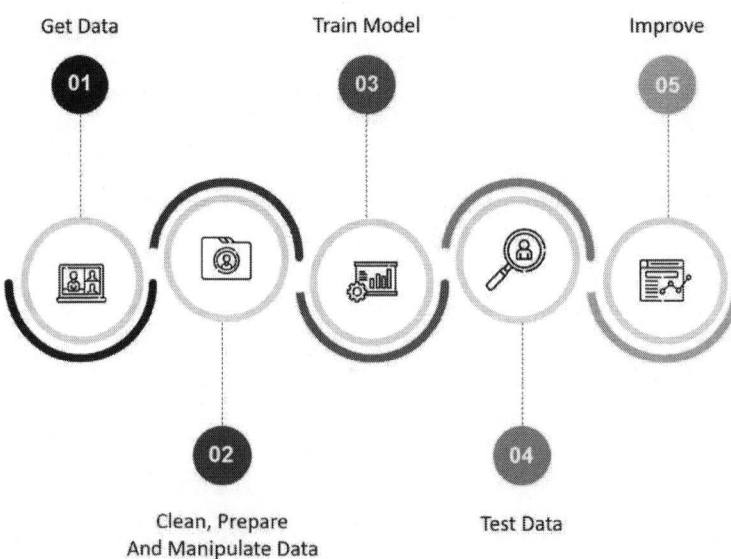

Figure 3.1 AI Pipeline

Recommendations

1. Invest in data literacy training programs for executives and key decision-makers to foster a data-driven culture within your organization.

2. Ensure compliance and governance frameworks are in place, safeguarding data quality and privacy.

3. Consider implementing a Chief Data Officer (CDO) role to oversee data management, strategy, and governance.

Leadership in the Age of Data and AI

There's a noticeable shift in executive roles and responsibilities with an increasing emphasis on data and AI transformation initiatives[2]. Many organizations are introducing the role of the Chief Data Officer (CDO), who often works in tandem with Chief Information Officers (CIOs) and other senior leaders. The CDO is responsible for overseeing and managing data-related responsibilities, ensuring alignment with broader business goals.

Trends in Data and AI Leadership

A 2021 NVP survey revealed a growing trend in executive roles centred around data. A significant 76% of respondents identified as either chief data officers or chief analytics officers[3]. This increasing importance and overlap of data and analytics roles in executive leadership indicate a broader recognition of the importance of data.

Future Trends in Data and AI

Looking ahead, the integration of AI and data analytics is expected to deepen. Technologies like Edge AI, Quantum Computing, and 5G will enhance data processing capabilities, further embedding the role of data in executive decision-making. Leaders should closely monitor these developments to maintain a competitive edge. Further insights will be explored in Chapter 25.

Conclusion

Understanding and championing the role of data is essential for executives in the age of AI. As technologies continue to evolve, executives with a deep understanding of data's potential will lead their organizations to success. In the next chapter, Chapter 4: The Indispensable Role of Data Literacy, we delve further into how data literacy equips executives to make more informed decisions in this complex landscape.

Footnotes

1. AI Ireland Interviews from 2018 to 2023 Insights

2. The Seven Roles of a Company's Chief Data Officer
https://hbr.org/webinar/2020/12/the-seven-roles-of-a-companys-chief-data-officer

3. NewVantage Partners Releases 2021 Big Data and AI Executive Survey
https://www.businesswire.com/news/home/20210104005022/en/NewVantage-Partners-Releases-2021-Big-Data-and-AI-Executive-Survey

4. Chapter 4:

The Indispensable Role of Data Literacy

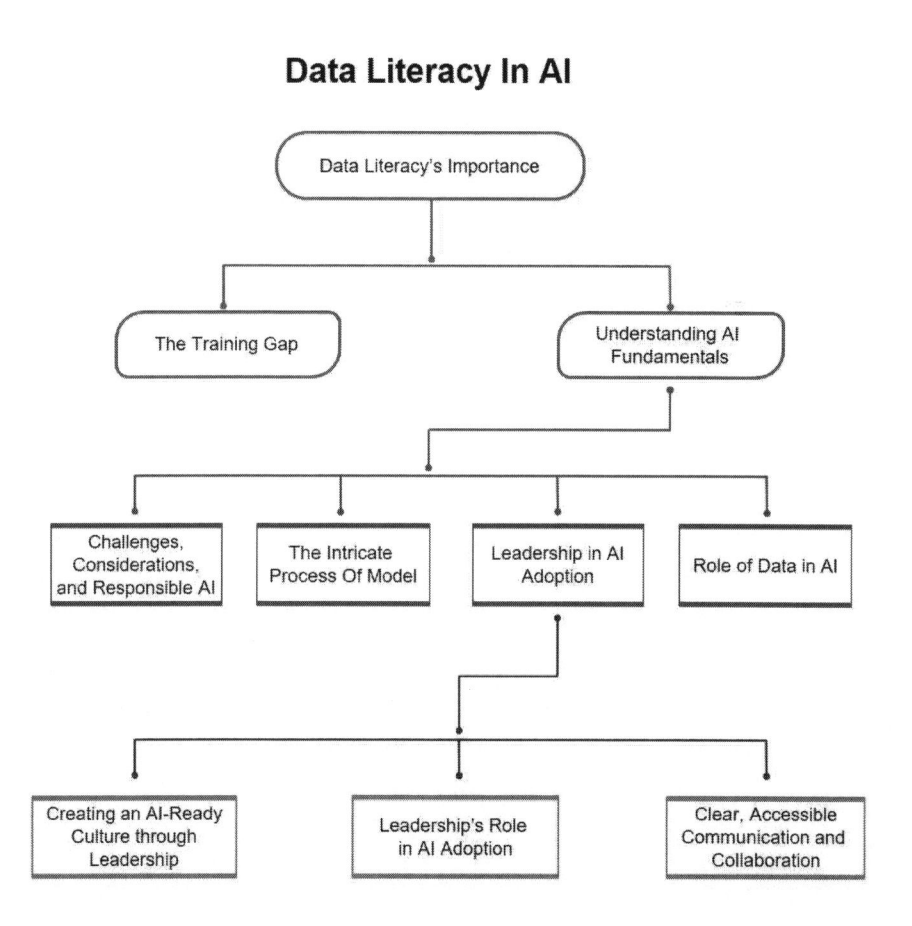

Figure 4.1 Data Literacy in AI

Key Takeaways

1. **Data Literacy's Significance:** Recognize the essential role of data literacy in contemporary organizations. Understand the existing training gap and the immediate applications of data-informed decisions.

2. **Decoding AI Basics:** Gain an in-depth understanding of the foundational elements of AI, including different types of data, data quality, and the intricacies involved in model training. Highlight challenges and ethical considerations.

3. **Leadership's Role in AI Integration:** Grasp the critical role senior management plays in spearheading AI transformation, cultivating an AI-adaptive culture, and guiding interdisciplinary teams effectively.

Introduction

In the era of the Fourth Industrial Revolution, data stands as the bedrock upon which contemporary businesses are built. The urgency for data literacy is escalating; projections indicate that by 2025, nearly 70% of the global workforce will engage with data, marking a significant uptick from 40% in 2018[1].

The Training Gap

The gap in data literacy is more than just a hurdle; it's a significant impediment to growth. As it stands, only 40% of employees feel adequately skilled to meet their employer's data demands[2]. Addressing this training gap is not just an HR issue; it's a strategic imperative.

Data Storytelling and Real-World Applications

The art of data storytelling holds the key to democratizing data across an organization. By translating intricate data sets into understandable narratives, companies can make informed decisions more efficiently.

The Multiple Facets of Data

Data comes in a myriad of formats: structured, unstructured, and semi-structured. While structured data facilitates straightforward analysis, unstructured data requires specialized algorithms and tools for interpretation.

Role of Data in AI

Data is the linchpin for all AI initiatives, acting as the raw material that fuels machine learning algorithms and predictive models. It's not merely the volume of data that matters, but also its quality, diversity, and integrity. High-quality data ensures that AI systems can make accurate predictions and decisions, while diverse datasets prevent biases and enhance the system's applicability across various scenarios. Ensuring data integrity is crucial for maintaining the trustworthiness and reliability of AI-driven solutions.

AI Ethics and Social Responsibility

Ethical considerations in AI are not mere add-ons; they are central to any AI deployment strategy. Organizations are obligated to follow governance frameworks that encompass data privacy, algorithmic fairness, and transparency. These frameworks serve as guiding principles to ensure that AI technologies are developed and applied in a manner that is socially responsible and aligned with ethical norms. Adherence to these guidelines is not just a legal necessity but also a cornerstone for building public trust in AI systems.

The Intricate Process of Model Training

Training a model is not a simple task of inputting data; it's a complex, iterative cycle involving learning, error correction, and validation. This rigorous process ensures that the AI system not only performs effectively but also operates within ethical and responsible boundaries. The quality of model training directly impacts the system's ability to make accurate predictions and decisions, making it a critical component in the deployment of any AI solution.

Challenges and Considerations

Recognizing the hurdles in model training is essential for responsible AI implementation. These challenges can range from resource limitations and intricate model complexities to the risk of ingrained biases. Addressing these issues head-on is vital for ensuring that the AI system is both effective and ethically sound.

The Role of Interdisciplinary Teams

AI is not just a technological venture but a comprehensive business transformation that calls for a multi-disciplinary team. This team should encompass specialists in data science, business strategy, ethical governance, and even psychology. Such a diverse group ensures that the AI initiative is not only technically sound but also ethically responsible and aligned with business objectives.

Leadership's Role in AI Adoption

The success of AI adoption hinges on proactive and committed leadership. This commitment extends beyond merely investing in technology; it also involves nurturing talent and optimizing processes. Effective leadership ensures that AI is seamlessly integrated into the organization's strategy, thereby maximizing its potential benefits.

Creating an AI-Ready Culture

Cultural adaptation is often the most challenging part of AI integration. Leaders must address potential resistance, which usually stems from concerns over job security or misunderstandings about the technology.

Author's Insight: The Human Factor in AI

In my in-depth conversations with a multitude of AI pioneers, a recurring yet frequently neglected theme is the human factor. The most impactful applications of AI are led by those who understand that this technology is not a substitute for human talent but a complement to it. These leaders recognize that AI serves to amplify human capabilities, creating a synergistic relationship that propels both technological and human advancement[3].

Recommendations:

1. **Invest in Data Literacy Programs:** Organizations should earmark budget and resources for targeted data literacy training initiatives.

2. **Ethical Governance:** Establish a robust governance framework that covers all facets of AI ethics.

3. **Role of Leadership:** Executives should prioritize transparent and continuous communication with their teams, especially when introducing new AI initiatives.

Conclusion

As we move to the next part of this book, the takeaways here underscore the essential elements necessary for effectively navigating the AI landscape: data literacy, a strong ethical framework, and committed leadership. The future trajectory of AI in businesses hinges on fostering data literacy, decoding AI complexities, and robust leadership. As we segue into Part Two of this book, "AI in Business Operations," Chapter 5 will focus on Return on Investment (ROI) from AI, providing executives with valuable metrics for evaluating AI initiatives.

Footnotes

1. "How CEOs Can Lead a Data-Driven Culture HBR By Thomas Davenport"

https://hbr.org/2020/03/how-ceos-can-lead-a-data-driven-culture

2. "The importance of Data Literacy and Data Storytelling by Bernard Marr" https://www.forbes.com/sites/bernardmarr/2022/09/28/the-importance-of-data-literacy-and-data-storytelling/

3. AI Ireland interview insights 2018 to 2023

Part 2

5. Chapter 5:

Return on Investment (ROI) from AI

Key Takeaways

1. Understand the challenges of introducing AI into an organization and their causes.

2. Learn how to calculate the ROI from AI projects, including typical KPIs, cost-benefit analysis, and evaluating both direct and indirect benefits.

3. Appreciate the nuanced value of ROI in AI, going beyond financial metrics to include strategic, long-term gains.

Introduction

Artificial Intelligence (AI) has become a strategic imperative for businesses across industries. However, the adoption of AI is not without its challenges. This chapter will delve into the hurdles organisations face when introducing AI, the causes behind these challenges, and how to calculate the ROI from AI projects.

Section 1: Challenges of AI Implementation in Enterprises.

1. Employee Training and Adaptability: A substantial 85% of the workforce expects that they will require training to adapt to the changes AI will bring to their job functions. This underscores the need for comprehensive educational programs that not only teach technical skills but also foster an understanding of how AI integrates into existing workflows[1].

2. **Data Quality and Relevance:** The success of AI systems hinges on the availability of high-quality and relevant data. Poor data quality can lead to inaccurate predictions and suboptimal decision-making. Organizations must invest in robust data governance frameworks to ensure data integrity[2].

3. **Organisational Resistance:** Resistance to AI adoption often arises from fears of job displacement or the perceived complexity of the technology. Addressing these concerns requires clear communication about the benefits of AI and how it will augment, rather than replace, human roles.

4. **Trust and Understanding:** Mistrust in AI systems can be a significant barrier to adoption. This often stems from a lack of understanding of how these systems operate. Transparency in AI operations, including explainable AI models and clear governance policies, is crucial for building trust. By addressing these challenges head-on, enterprises can pave the way for more effective and responsible AI implementation.

5. **Data Privacy and Security:** As AI systems process large volumes of data, the issue of data privacy and the risk of data breaches become increasingly important. Organisations must adhere to stringent data protection regulations and invest in secure data storage solutions.

6. **Talent Shortage:** The demand for skilled AI professionals far outstrips supply, making talent acquisition a significant challenge. Companies may need to invest in training existing staff or partnering with educational institutions to bridge this gap.
7. **Cost Implications:** The financial investment required for AI implementation can be substantial, covering not just technology but also employee training and ongoing maintenance.
8. **Measuring ROI:** Quantifying the return on investment for AI initiatives can be complex, particularly in the early stages. Organizations need to establish clear metrics and KPIs to evaluate success.
9. **Integration Challenges:** Seamlessly integrating AI solutions into existing systems and workflows requires careful planning and technical expertise. Failure to do so can result in operational disruptions.
10. **Regulatory and Compliance Issues:** Compliance with international and local regulations is essential to avoid legal repercussions. This includes not only data protection laws but also industry-specific regulations.

Addressing these additional challenges requires a multifaceted approach, involving strategic planning, resource allocation, and continuous monitoring to ensure successful and responsible AI deployment.

Section 2: Causes of these Challenges.

1. **Organizational Culture:** A company's existing culture may be resistant to change, making it difficult to integrate AI technologies.

Employees may be wary of AI's impact on job security, leading to resistance.
2. **Technical Limitations:** Outdated or incompatible systems can create bottlenecks in the AI integration process. The lack of modern infrastructure can limit the capabilities of AI applications.
3. **Financial Constraints:** Budget limitations can restrict the scope of AI projects, affecting both the quality of the technology and the training required for effective implementation.
4. **Regulatory Environment:** Rapidly evolving laws and regulations around data privacy and AI ethics can complicate deployment strategies. Organizations must stay abreast of legal changes to ensure compliance.

Section 3: Calculating ROI from AI Projects.

Calculating ROI from AI projects is not merely a financial exercise; it's a comprehensive evaluation that encompasses both tangible and intangible benefits. Establishing key performance indicators (KPIs) at the project's outset provides a baseline for future comparison. These KPIs should be aligned with organizational goals and monitored regularly to assess the project's ongoing impact. By combining these metrics, organizations can achieve a holistic understanding of their AI project's ROI.

1. **Quantifiable Returns**: This encompasses financial growth, expense reductions, and other quality-based outcomes.
2. **Operational Productivity**: AI can streamline tasks, resulting in the conservation of time and resources.

3. **Mitigation of Risks**: Through predictive analysis, potential challenges can be pinpointed.

4. **Enhancement of Revenue**: AI can augment the number of consumers and guide the creation of products.

5. **Long-term Strategic Returns**: This focuses on the contribution of AI in realizing enduring organizational ambitions.

Author's Insight: The ROI Paradox in AI

Evaluating the ROI of AI is not solely about immediate financial gains; it also considers long-term strategic advantages. CarTrawler, a company that designs and implements custom car rental and mobility solutions, serves as a case in point. Initially, they encountered various challenges, ranging from testing limitations to reservations about full-scale automation. Despite these hurdles, they persisted in developing a comprehensive machine learning infrastructure. As a result, they have not only increased their revenue but also enhanced their market position, with over 15 machine learning models now in active operation. This has allowed them to focus on their core offerings while still owning the 'last mile' for their customers[3].

Recommendations

1. Organizations should invest in data literacy programs: To ensure that employees can effectively navigate and utilize AI technologies, companies should allocate resources to comprehensive data literacy training. This will not only enhance the skill set of the workforce but also contribute to the successful deployment of AI projects.

2. A clear understanding of ROI metrics specific to AI projects should be established: Companies need to develop a set of key performance indicators (KPIs) tailored to AI initiatives. This will enable them to measure the success of their projects more accurately and make data-driven decisions.

3. C-suite executives must take an active role in AI initiatives for effective integration: Leadership involvement is crucial for the successful adoption of AI. Executives should not only provide financial backing but also actively participate in strategy development and implementation processes. Their commitment will serve as a catalyst for organizational change and AI adoption.

Conclusion

The journey toward AI adoption is fraught with complexities, yet the potential benefits are pivotal for business success. As we transition to the next chapter, we will explore the transformative impact of AI on customer experience, offering another lens through which to evaluate ROI. For those seeking a practical approach to quantifying AI's value, a comprehensive ROI checklist is included in the appendix.

Footnotes

1. " Jobs On The Verge Of Disruption: How Is AI Set To Redefine The Workforce? "
https://www.forbes.com/sites/byroncole/2023/08/09/jobs-on-the-verge-of-disruption-how-is-ai-set-to-redefine-the-workforce/

2. "Re-Thinking Data Strategy and Integration for Artificial Intelligence: " https://www.mdpi.com/2076-3417/13/12/7082#:~:text=Low%2Dquality%20data%20can%20lead,produce%20reliable%20and%20valuable%20results.

3. "Cartrawler and AI Ireland Webinar "
https://www.youtube.com/watch?v=gWC0QO2b-2Q

Executive Checklist for Calculating ROI on AI Projects is in the Appendix

6. Chapter 6:

AI and Customer Experience

Key Takeaways

1. **AI's Dual-Edged Sword**: While AI offers personalized and efficient customer experiences, there are concerns about data privacy and the potential loss of the human touch in customer interactions.

2. **Customer-Centric AI**: The primary goal of AI in customer service should always be to enhance customer satisfaction and loyalty, rather than just short-term gains.

3. **Empowering Employees with AI**: Integrating AI into standard operating procedures can help employees serve customers better, but human oversight remains crucial.

Figure 6.1 AI In Customer Service

Introduction

As discussed in Chapter 5, AI is significantly transforming various industries. In the realm of customer experience, AI's potential is vast, yet it brings a host of concerns, particularly in sectors like healthcare and banking where data privacy is paramount.

Section 1: The Potential and Risks of AI

6..1. The Promise of AI

Building upon the insights from Chapter 5, it becomes evident that AI is not merely a technological advancement, but a catalyst for transformation across various industries. As we shift our attention to the realm of customer experience, the potential of AI is both vast and intricate. While the technology offers immense promise for personalising interactions and streamlining services, it also introduces a host of complex issues. This is particularly true in sectors like healthcare and banking, where the importance of data privacy is paramount. In this chapter, we shall delve into the multifaceted impact of AI on customer experience, weighing its potential advantages against the ethical considerations it demands.

6..2. The Risk of Misplaced Priorities

Companies risk losing focus on long-term customer loyalty as they chase quick gains through AI. Businesses need to ensure that the deployment of AI augments the customer experience, not detracts from it.

Section 2: The Centrality of Customer Love

6..1. Every Interaction Matters

In the context of AI-driven customer experience, the significance of each customer interaction cannot be overstated. Each touchpoint serves as an opportunity to either reinforce long-term loyalty or risk diminishing customer satisfaction. Leveraging AI allows businesses to make these interactions more meaningful, personalised, and efficient, thereby elevating the overall customer experience.

6..2. Enriching Customers' Lives

The ultimate goal for businesses is to enrich the lives of their customers. Preliminary studies suggest that AI has the capacity to not only streamline operations but also to elevate customer satisfaction and bolster employee retention rates. By integrating AI into customer experience strategies, companies can offer more personalised and efficient services, thereby positively impacting various facets of the customer's life. For instance, in the healthcare industry, AI-powered chatbots are being used to provide immediate responses to patient queries, thereby improving patient satisfaction and freeing up medical staff to focus on more complex tasks

Section 3: Personalizing the Customer Experience

The advent of AI has opened up new avenues for personalising customer experiences, making it possible to tailor services and products to individual preferences and behaviours.

6..1. Rethinking Objective Functions

The primary aim of AI should be to augment customer satisfaction. The focus of AI applications needs to transition from merely achieving short-term objectives to a model that continually learns and evolves based on customer interactions. For example, in the retail industry, AI algorithms are increasingly being used to optimise inventory based on real-time customer behaviour rather than just historical sales data.

6..2. The Power of Personalization

Customers increasingly desire personalised experiences and are willing to share personal data to achieve this, provided they have trust in the service provider. For instance, in the streaming services industry, platforms like Netflix use AI to analyse viewing habits and preferences to recommend shows and movies, thereby enhancing user engagement and satisfaction.

Author's Insight

In a podcast interview with Bart Lehane, CTO of EdgeTier, we delved into the transformative impact of their AI technology on customer engagement. EdgeTier's sophisticated AI platform streamlines the organisation and management of customer conversations, thereby allowing customer service agents to concentrate on meaningful interactions. A particularly noteworthy feature is the real-time "anomaly detection," which swiftly identifies critical issues such as customer complaints or potentially fraudulent activities. This suite of tools empowers businesses to deliver exceptional response times without compromising the indispensable human element[1].

Case Study 1: Leveraging AI to Monitor Customer Sentiment on Social Media

In today's digital age, the sheer volume of social media activity makes it increasingly challenging for businesses to manually monitor customer sentiment. Coca-Cola, a leading global brand, has tackled this issue by deploying AI algorithms that continuously scan social media platforms for mentions related to their brand. The AI system is sophisticated enough to identify not only the company's name but also specific products and even common misspellings.

Upon detecting a mention, the algorithm categorises it as either positive, negative, or neutral. Any critical or negative mentions immediately trigger an alert to the customer service team. Within minutes, a customer service representative engages with the concerned individual to resolve the issue. This proactive approach has yielded impressive results: a 20% uptick in customer satisfaction and a 25% reduction in customer churn rates[2]. Most significantly, the AI system helped Coca-Cola identify a design flaw in one of their top-selling products, leading to a product redesign that subsequently boosted sales by 15%[3].

Case Study 2: Domino's Pizza and the AI-Driven Customer Service

Domino's Pizza has taken customer service to the next level with their AI-driven chatbot, "Dom." Far from being just an order-taking interface, Dom offers personalized product recommendations based on a variety of factors such as past orders, ongoing promotions, and even weather conditions. For instance, on a chilly day, Dom might suggest adding a hot chocolate or a warm dessert to your order.

Beyond order placement and tracking, Dom serves as a comprehensive customer service tool, capable of answering frequently asked questions about ingredients, delivery policies, and more. Operating 24/7, the chatbot significantly eases the workload on human customer service agents, allowing them to focus on resolving more complex customer issues. What sets Dom apart is its capacity for continuous learning.

Domino's regularly updates the chatbot based on customer feedback and usage patterns, ensuring it remains a valuable asset in enhancing customer experience. The results speak for themselves: a 30% increase in online orders and a 20% boost in customer satisfaction scores[4.] A recent survey revealed that 80% of customers who interacted with Dom found it "very helpful," and 70% indicated they would use the service again[4].

Recommendations

1. **Invest in Data Security:** With more data collection, companies should fortify their data security measures to protect customer information.

2. **Regular Training:** Employees should undergo periodic training to effectively use AI tools and understand their limitations.

3. **Customer Feedback Loop**: Always maintain a feedback loop to continually refine and improve the AI tools in customer service applications.

Conclusion

As we conclude this chapter, it's evident that AI's role in customer service is not just transformative but pivotal. While the technological advancements, particularly in generative AI—which we will delve into in Chapter 7—offer unprecedented opportunities for business enhancement, the ultimate measure of success remains customer satisfaction. Companies must not lose sight of this fundamental principle as they integrate AI into their customer service strategies.

The case studies of Coca-Cola and Domino's Pizza underscore the tangible benefits of a customer-centric AI approach, from increased customer satisfaction to reduced churn rates. These real-world applications serve as a roadmap for other enterprises looking to leverage AI effectively. As we move forward, the focus should not just be on what AI can do, but on how it can enrich the customer experience while adhering to ethical and data privacy standards.

In the next chapter, we will explore how generative AI can further revolutionize customer interactions, opening new avenues for personalized and efficient service. However, as we adopt these advanced technologies, the emphasis must always be on enhancing customer satisfaction, the cornerstone of any successful business.

Footnotes

1. AI Ireland Edgetier Bart Lehane interview
    https://aiawards.ie/e21-bart-lehane-edgetier-2/

2. " The future of Costumer Service: An Inside Look at Zendesk AI"
https://tollanis.com/leadership-and-insights/the-future-of-customer-service-an-inside-look-at-zendesk-ai/

3. Coca-Cola case study AI
    https://www.almabetter.com/bytes/articles/case-study-of-coca-cola

4. The Secret Surveillance Sauce to Domino Pizza's Success
    https://d3.harvard.edu/platform-digit/submission/the-secret-surveillance-sauce-to-dominos-success/

7. Chapter 7:

In-depth Look at Generative AI for Business

Key Takeaways

1. Generative AI is not just a technological shift; it's an operational transformation that is already having a significant impact across multiple industries.

2. Decision-makers need to consider the technology's broader implications, focusing on its quality, diversity, and speed.

3. Adopting Generative AI is not a straightforward process; it involves strategic planning, investment in skills, risk management, and a deep understanding of ethical considerations.

Introduction to Generative AI

In Chapter 6, we examined AI's role in customer service. Now, we shift focus to Generative AI, a field gaining prominence since OpenAI's ChatGPT launch in November 2022. Unlike traditional AI, which excels in analytics and decision-making, Generative AI creates new content, from text to multimedia. This technology is swiftly moving from experimental to mainstream, propelled by advanced algorithms and neural networks.

Innovations like Generative Adversarial Networks (GANs) have expanded Generative AI's capabilities. Tools like ChatGPT employ these models to create adaptive machine learning systems. However, the rise of Generative AI also poses ethical challenges, such as the creation of deepfakes. As computational power grows, Generative AI's applications and impact are set to broaden. This chapter explores its current state, future potential, and the ethical considerations that accompany its growth[1].

Evaluating Generative AI Model

The critical factors for evaluating generative AI models remain quality, diversity, and speed. Companies should also consider the reliability and robustness of the model in different operational environments.

Real-World Applications of Generative AI

Generative AI is making transformative impacts across various sectors, offering innovative and efficient solutions. Goldman Sachs research in April 2023 predicted Generative AI could raise global GDP by 7% which is almost 7 trillion dollars over a 10-year period[2]. Here are some industry-specific applications, complemented by case studies to provide a more comprehensive view:

Healthcare

1. Accelerated Drug Development

Generative AI is expediting the drug discovery process by creating candidates for clinical trials. This initiative gained traction when Exscientia introduced an AI-formulated drug into clinical trials in 2021.

2. Advancements in Genetic Research

Generative AI is aiding researchers in understanding gene expression changes, thereby accelerating gene therapy development and enhancing treatment effectiveness[3].

3. Precision in Medical Imaging

Generative AI is improving the accuracy of medical imaging techniques like CT scans, aiding in more precise diagnoses.

Fashion

4. Innovative Design Solutions

Tools like Dall-e are enabling designers to generate realistic and creative fashion designs, keeping pace with industry trends.

5. Virtual Fashion Models

Generative AI simplifies the complexities of photoshoots and model selection by creating virtual 3D models to showcase clothing.

6. Market and Trend Analytics

Generative AI analyzes customer preferences to offer personalized product recommendations and informs targeted marketing strategies.

Education

7. Tailored Educational Programs

Generative AI customizes lesson plans based on student performance, making education more effective and personalized.

Additional Sectors Benefiting from Generative AI

8. **Manufacturing:** Enhanced product design and predictive maintenance.

9. **Agriculture:** Optimized crop management and accurate weather forecasting.

10. **Finance:** Automated customer service and data-driven investment strategies.

11. **Education:** Personalized learning experiences and automated assignment assistance.

12. Text Generation for Customized Content Creation

Platforms like ChatGPT can produce grammatically correct and contextually relevant text, aiding businesses in crafting marketing materials. Users can further tailor this content by specifying its type, target audience, and tone.

13. Automating Code Generation and Quality Assurance

Generative AI tools like ChatGPT can generate precise code for specific tasks, streamlining the software development process. These platforms also offer code review, debugging, refactoring, and style checks, enhancing code quality.

By understanding the practical applications and case studies of Generative AI, businesses and institutions can better leverage its capabilities for innovation and efficiency.

Limitations of Generative AI

Generative AI is still in its nascent stages and comes with its own set of limitations that businesses need to be aware of:

1. Data Quality and Bias: Any AI system is only as good as the data it consumes. Biases or errors in the data can be reflected in the generated content.

2. Lack of Original Research: AI can't conduct original research or deep analysis. The content it generates is generally surface level.

3. Fact-Checking Required: AI-generated content may contain inaccuracies and should be fact-checked.

4. **No Lived Experience:** AI can mimic human language but can't replicate lived experiences, which are crucial for certain types of content.

5. Quality Control: AI can generate text logically, but taste and quality are not accounted for. Human intervention is essential for quality control.

Generative AI in Business: Insights from KPMG Survey August 2023

A recent survey by KPMG highlighted the growing significance of generative AI in the business world. The survey found that 97% of US executives believe generative AI will have a high impact on their organizations in the next 12-18 months[4]. Moreover, 80% think it will disrupt their industry, and 93% see its value for their business[4]. Those who have already adopted generative AI tools are more optimistic about its impact, foreseeing significant disruption in their industries and expecting more value from it. However, concerns about the uncertain regulatory environment remain a barrier to its implementation.

Recommendations for Overcoming Limitations:

1. Human-AI Collaboration: Use AI as a tool rather than a replacement for human skills. Writers and editors should focus on bringing depth, quality control, and editorial strategy to AI-generated content.

2. **Data Auditing:** Regularly audit the data used to train AI models to ensure it is free from biases and errors.

3. Quality Assurance Processes: Implement robust QA processes to fact-check and improve the quality of AI-generated content.

4. **Ethical Guidelines**: Develop ethical guidelines specifically addressing the limitations and potential biases of using Generative AI.

5. **Continuous Learning and Adaptation:** As Generative AI evolves businesses should adapt by updating their strategies and guidelines accordingly.

Recommendations for Implementing Generative AI:

1. **Investment in Skillset**: Organizations should not overlook the importance of upskilling their staff. Comprehensive training programs are key to ensuring smooth transitions and optimal utilization of generative AI.

2. **Robust Risk Management**: Risk mitigation plans must include ongoing monitoring and evaluation components. Utilize third-party audits and certifications to ensure compliance with industry standards.

3. **Ethical Guidelines**: Ethics should not be an afterthought; companies need to embed ethical considerations into their AI strategies right from the planning stage.

4. **Pilot Testing:** Pilot tests should be multi-phased, starting with closed environments before transitioning to real-world settings. The feedback loop should be strong to make necessary adjustments during this stage.

Impact on the Workforce

Generative AI, while promising efficiency, may lead to a workforce displacement if not managed carefully. Organizations must prepare for this by creating alternative job roles and reskilling programs.

Author's Insight and Summary

Based on comprehensive research, corroborated by the McKinsey Global Survey[5] and an enlightening discussion with Kieran McCorry from Microsoft[6], it is clear that the growth of generative AI is unparalleled. Organizations leading in AI implementation are outpacing their rivals, largely due to the sophisticated functionalities offered by generative AI.

For example, Microsoft has integrated "copilots" into their software suite, a feature powered by generative AI. This innovation aids users in various tasks, such as crafting PowerPoint slides or programming, thereby optimizing the creative workflow, conserving time, and enabling users to concentrate on more strategic activities.

In a recent interview with Mark Dunleavy, the Country Manager of Amazon Web Services (AWS) Ireland, he emphasized the need for education to demystify generative AI. He stated, "The conversation around Generative AI is just beginning; the ship has not yet left the harbor. It's crucial to distinguish between Generative AI and other forms of AI, as the former has not garnered as much attention as the latter, despite its transformative potential[7]."

Conclusion

Generative AI represents an exciting frontier for business innovation. However, its rapid adoption also necessitates a well-thought-out approach. Businesses need to invest in pilot projects, partnerships, and research to fully comprehend its far-reaching implications. In our next Chapter we will discuss how AI is being used within sales and marketing.

Footnotes

1. "PMG Survey: Momentum for Generative AI Continues to Build in Organizations" https://www.techrepublic.com/article/kpmg-survey-generative-ai-2023/#:~:text=A%20newly%20released%20study%20by,the%20top%20emerging%20enterprise%20technology.

2. Goldman Sachs Survey Generative AI could raise global GDP by 7%

https://www.goldmansachs.com/intelligence/pages/generative-ai-could-raise-global-gdp-by-7-percent.html

3.Leveraging AI Models To Improve Safety of Gene Therapy
https://www.formbio.com/blog/ai-generative-models-gene-therapy

4.Generative AI in Business: Insights from KPMG Survey August 2023   https://advisory-marketing.us.kpmg.com/speed/genai2023.html

5. The State of AI in 2023
   https://www.mckinsey.com/capabilities/quantumblack/our-insights/the-state-of-ai-in-2023-generative-ais-breakout-year

6. AI Ireland Microsoft Kieran McCorry AI Podcast 2023
https://aiireland.ie/2023/06/22/unleashing-the-power-of-generative-ai-kieran-mccorry/

7. AI Ireland Interview AWS Global Logic To be released October 2023

8. Chapter 8:

AI in Marketing and Sales

Key Takeaways

1. AI is a strategic differentiator in marketing and sales, offering automation, process optimization, and data-driven decision-making capabilities.

2. Real-world examples from Nutella and Volkswagen illustrate the transformative potential of AI across various marketing and sales functions.

3. Successful AI adoption requires strategic alignment, continuous learning, ethical considerations, and a balance between AI and human interaction.

Introduction

In Chapter 7, we covered Generative AI and some of its applications across business. The explosive growth of generative AI tools is reshaping the marketing and sales landscape, with 40% of organizations planning to increase their investment in AI due to advances in generative AI[1].

The Strategic Imperative of AI in Marketing and Sales

In the fiercely competitive business landscape, Artificial Intelligence (AI) is no longer just a technological tool; it's a strategic imperative that's reshaping the marketing and sales sectors. By deciphering complex customer data, AI can unearth valuable insights into buying patterns and preferences, empowering businesses to tailor their marketing campaigns and boost conversions.

Case Studies: Real-World Applications

8..1. Nutella: Personalized Marketing Campaigns

Nutella leveraged AI to create a highly successful personalized marketing campaign. Using machine learning algorithms, the company analysed customer data to understand purchasing behaviour and preferences. This data was then used to generate unique label designs for Nutella jars. Each design was algorithmically created to appeal to different customer segments, making each jar of Nutella a unique product. The campaign led to a significant increase in sales and customer engagement, showcasing the power of AI in creating highly personalized marketing strategies[2].

8..2. Volkswagen: AI-Driven Ad Buying

Volkswagen utilized AI to revolutionize its advertising strategy. The company employed machine learning algorithms to automate its ad-buying decisions. These algorithms analysed real-time data on ad performance, customer engagement, and market trends to make instant decisions on where to place ads for maximum impact. This AI-driven approach led to more cost-effective campaign investments and a 20% increase in sales[3].

8..3. Strategic Alignment: The Key to AI Success in Marketing and Sales

For executives, the key to unlocking the power of AI lies in strategic alignment. This involves defining clear goals, identifying areas where AI can add the most value, and selecting the right AI solutions. It's also crucial to invest in training employees on how to use AI tools and technologies effectively.

8..4. AI-Enabled Marketing: Personalization at Its Best

AI's ability to analyse and learn from data enables it to create highly personalized marketing content. This capability extends from crafting tailored emails to different customer segments to generating unique product packaging designs.

8..5. AI in Sales: Enhancing Customer Engagement and Efficiency

In sales, AI can assist with lead qualification, product demonstrations, and customer engagement. AI-generated sales representatives can interact with customers, analyse data, and perform tasks typically carried out by human salespeople.

Author's Insights

AI is a game-changer in sales and marketing, and its impact is further amplified by Generative AI tools like ChatGPT and Bard. These tools enhance customer engagement and automate tasks, offering a competitive edge. Kieran McCorry from Microsoft highlighted that Azure Open AI can unlock new business insights but emphasized responsible use[4]. AI is streamlining customer interactions through chatbots, optimizing pricing, and automating routine tasks. The inclusion of Generative AI tools like ChatGPT and Bard takes this to the next level by offering more personalized and interactive customer experiences.

Recommendations

1. Training: Invest in training programs to help your team understand how to use AI tools effectively.

2. Data Quality: Ensure the data used for AI algorithms is of high quality to avoid biases and inaccuracies.

3. Ethical Guidelines: Establish ethical guidelines for AI usage, particularly concerning data privacy and customer engagement.

Ethical and Privacy Considerations in AI Adoption

When integrating AI into marketing and sales, it's important to consider the ethical and privacy implications. The adoption of AI in sales and marketing comes with its own set of ethical and privacy challenges that organizations must navigate to maintain consumer trust and regulatory compliance.

8..1. Data Privacy

AI-driven marketing strategies often rely on customer data. Ensuring the secure and ethical handling of this data is paramount. Companies must comply with regulations like GDPR and offer transparent data usage policies.

8..2. Algorithmic Bias

AI algorithms can inadvertently perpetuate biases present in their training data, affecting the fairness of marketing strategies. Organisations should employ fairness-aware modelling to mitigate such risks.

8..3. Transparency

Transparency is key in AI applications for sales and marketing. Companies should be clear about how AI algorithms make decisions, especially in customer targeting and personalization.

8..4. Consumer Consent

Providing consumers with clear opt-out options for data collection and AI-driven personalization is essential for ethical compliance and building trust.

By addressing these ethical and privacy considerations, companies can responsibly leverage AI in sales and marketing, aligning with both legal requirements and consumer expectations.

Conclusion: Striking the Right Balance

AI is reshaping business, especially in sales and marketing through Generative AI tools like ChatGPT and Bard. However, responsible use is key, as emphasized by Kieran McCorry from Microsoft[4]. As we transition from discussing AI in sales and marketing in Chapter 8 to pinpointing AI opportunities in the next chapter, it's crucial to balance AI with human interaction and align initiatives with company values and regulations.

Footnotes

1. McKinsey Survey The State of AI in 2023 https://www.mckinsey.com/capabilities/quantumblack/our-insights/the-state-of-ai-in-2023-generative-ais-breakout-year

2. An Algorithm Designed 7 Million One-Of-A-Kind Labels for a Nutella Campaign

https://futurism.com/an-algorithm-designed-7-million-one-of-a-kind-labels-for-a-nutella-campaign

3. How Volkswagen is using artificial intellience for ad buying decisions. https://mediamakersmeet.com/how-volkswagen-is-using-artificial-intelligence-for-ad-buying-decisions/#:~:text=Cars%20aren't%20the%20only,effective%20than%20its%20media%20agency.

4. E104 Kieran McCorry National Technology Manager at Microsoft AI Ireland Interview

https://www.youtube.com/watch?v=CKdm8TyKKiE

9. Chapter 9:

Pinpointing AI Opportunities within your Business

Key Takeaways:

1. Alignment with Business Goals: Ensure that your AI initiatives align perfectly with your broader business objectives for seamless integration and stakeholder buy-in.

2. Effective Project Management: Oversee your AI projects meticulously from start to finish, ensuring that you have clear goals, timelines, and resource allocations.

3. Ethical AI: Always consider the ethical implications of your AI initiatives to build trust and avoid legal issues.

Introduction

After delving into AI's impact on sales and marketing in Chapter 8 and exploring Generative AI, Chapter 9 shifts focus to identifying AI opportunities within your organization. To fully leverage AI's transformative potential, this chapter will guide you in pinpointing areas where AI can add the most value—be it in efficiency, decision-making, or innovation.

Identifying AI Opportunities in Your Business

A thorough analysis should cover all organizational facets, from customer service and marketing to HR and supply chain management.

Look for repetitive tasks ripe for automation, decisions that could benefit from predictive analytics, and data-rich areas that can yield valuable insights.

Aligning AI Initiatives with Business Goals

AI projects should align with broader business objectives. This means setting clear goals for your AI initiatives and ensuring they're integrated across departments. Such integration promotes smoother implementation, cross-departmental collaboration, and prevents isolated silos. Stakeholders buy-in is also pivotal for success.

Managing AI Projects

Overseeing AI projects involves several key steps, from inception to maintenance. This includes clear goal setting, timeline establishment, team assembly, and resource allocation. Effective communication, collaboration, and risk management are vital during the execution phase. It's equally important to track progress and manage changes effectively.

Monitoring and Evaluating AI Project Success

Defining success metrics that align with business goals is essential. This could range from efficiency improvements and error reductions to sales boosts or enhanced customer experiences. Implement robust monitoring mechanisms and establish regular evaluations and feedback loops for continuous refinement.

Checklist for Pinpointing AI Opportunities

To aid your AI implementation journey, a comprehensive checklist can guide you in identifying AI opportunities that align with business goals and result in tangible improvements. This checklist, available in the Appendix, covers areas like business analysis, data assessment, technology readiness, and more.

Author's Insights

In my interviews with industry leaders, it's clear that pinpointing AI opportunities can yield significant benefits across various sectors. For example, a supply chain executive shared that AI helped cut costs by 20% through optimised routing and stock management[1]. In customer service, AI chatbots not only improved satisfaction rates but also freed up staff for more complex issues. A healthcare leader highlighted how AI algorithms have been a game-changer in diagnosing and treating patients more accurately[1]. In manufacturing, AI-driven quality checks have increased production speed and reduced errors. A retail executive noted a revenue boost thanks to AI's role in personalised marketing[1]. From the financial sector, AI's role in fraud detection has been pivotal in risk management[1]. Lastly, a tech leader emphasised how AI accelerates innovation, shortening the time-to-market for new products. The leaders who are successful at introducing AI within their business understand the importance of identifying the right AI opportunities to maximise benefits while aligning with company values and regulations.

Recommendations

1. **Start Small, Think Big**: Begin with pilot projects to test the waters. Once you've gained some experience and data, scale your efforts. Pilot projects allow you to make mistakes on a smaller scale, learn from them, and refine your strategy before rolling it out across the organization.

2. **Cross-Functional Teams**: Include members from various departments to ensure that the AI project aligns with overall business objectives. A diverse team brings multiple perspectives and can identify potential pitfalls or opportunities that may not be apparent to a homogenous group.

3. **Ethical Considerations:** Always consider the ethical implications of your AI projects, especially in terms of data privacy and job displacement. Ethical AI not only protects your company from legal repercussions but also builds trust with your customers and stakeholders.

Conclusion

AI offers transformative potential for businesses. By pinpointing AI opportunities, aligning them with business goals, managing projects effectively, and continuously monitoring their success, businesses can harness AI as a potent tool for growth and innovation. In Chapter 10: we will discuss how to leverage AI in Small and Medium Businesses (SMBs)

Footnotes

1. AI Ireland interviews 2018-2023

10. Chapter 10:

Leveraging AI in Small and Medium Businesses (SMBs): Driving Growth and Innovation

Key Takeaways

1. **AI's Growing Role in SMBs:** AI technologies, once exclusive to large corporations, are now driving success in small businesses.

2. **Overcoming AI Challenges:** Despite challenges like resource constraints and data privacy, the benefits of AI, such as enhanced productivity and reduced errors, are transformative for SMB's.

3. **Real-World AI Applications:** Practical AI tools, from computer vision in stock management to data analytics in inventory, are revolutionizing SMB operations.

Introduction

In Chapter 9, we explored how to identify AI opportunities within your organisation. Chapter 10 shifts the focus to the application of AI in Small and Medium Businesses (SMBs). This chapter delves into both the opportunities and challenges that SMBs face when adopting AI, providing practical guidance for their AI journey. Recent advancements, particularly in Generative AI, have made AI more accessible than ever for small business owners.

Section 1: The Current State of AI in SMBs

A recent study from Deloitte and Stanford University reveals that 25% of small businesses are currently using AI in some form, such as chatbots, predictive analytics, and marketing automation[1]. This indicates that AI is becoming increasingly accessible and relevant for SMBs. However, it also suggests that a significant proportion of SMBs are yet to tap into the potential of AI, highlighting the need for more education and support in this area.

Another survey conducted by Constant Contact in conjunction with market research firm Ascend, as reported in Forbes, shows that 91% of small businesses using AI indicate that it has made their business more successful[2]. This underscores the fact that AI is not just for large businesses anymore. The study also found a strong correlation between a small company's use of AI and its overall success.

Section 2: The Benefits of AI for SMBs

AI delivers numerous upsides to small businesses, revolutionising their day-to-day functions.

In this section, we'll spotlight key areas where AI can make a real difference for small businesses. By understanding these upsides, small business owners can better target where AI will have the most impact. Armed with the right know-how and tools, integrating AI becomes a practical and achievable goal.

10..1. Subsection 2.1: Streamlining and Automating Processes

AI excels at taking over routine tasks, allowing staff to concentrate on strategic work. This boosts efficiency and cuts costs. According to a Constant Contact survey, 28% of small business owners anticipate AI will save them at least $5,000 in the next year[2]. The starting point is simple: business owners should list manual tasks ripe for automation and ask, "What insights could enhance my business?"

10..2. Subsection 2.2: Enhancing Productivity and Innovation

AI not only offers data-driven insights but also fosters innovation and productivity. Russ Morton, Chief Product Officer of Constant Contact, highlights the advances in natural language processing and large language models. These technologies enable two-way dialogues with algorithms, transforming how tech processes data and generates content. An example could be AI-powered content creation tools that draft marketing copy or generate social media posts, making the creative process more efficient and tailored to the audience.

10..3. Subsection 2.3: Improving Work Quality and Saving Time

AI can significantly elevate work quality by minimising errors and ensuring consistency. It's also a time-saver, offering quick responses to customer questions. Small business owners report key benefits such as time savings, fewer manual errors, and accelerated growth. A real-world example could be an AI-powered inventory management system. This system not only keeps track of stock levels automatically but also predicts future inventory needs based on past data, thereby reducing manual errors and saving time that can be used for business growth strategies.

Section 3: Challenges of Implementing AI in SMBs

While AI brings a host of advantages, its adoption in small businesses isn't without hurdles.

In the following section, we'll explore some of these challenges in detail, offering insights to help SMB owners navigate the complexities of AI implementation.

10..1. Subsection 3.1: Lack of Resources

SMBs typically operate with constrained resources, making it challenging to invest in AI technology and the required expertise. Additionally, allocating resources to a novel concept like AI can be hard to justify without clear, immediate returns. These limitations often pose significant barriers to AI adoption for small businesses.

10..2. Subsection 3.2: Data Privacy and Security Concerns

Implementing AI usually requires handling vast volumes of data, raising concerns about data privacy and security. Many SMB owners lack the expertise to navigate these complex issues, making it a significant hurdle in AI adoption. This skill and knowledge gap can deter small businesses from fully leveraging the benefits of AI.

10..3. Subsection 3.3: Skills Gap and Learning Curve

Implementing AI requires specific skills and expertise, which may not be readily available in SMBs. The perceived cost, the learning curve, and a beginner's understanding of AI benefits are among the top obstacles for those interested in AI but are not currently using it.

Section 4: AI Applications for SMBs

AI holds the potential for diverse applications within SMBs, offering a range of significant benefits. In the subsequent section of this chapter, we will delve into some of these practical applications, providing insights to help small business owners make the most of AI in their operations.

10..1. Subsection 4.1: Customer Service Automation

With the use of chatbots and customer service automation, businesses can offer faster and more efficient customer service. For instance, 1-800-Flowers, a floral retailer, successfully incorporates AI-powered chatbots to improve customer service and boost sales. Similarly, Sephora employs AI chatbots to provide personalised product recommendations to online shoppers based on their skin type and preferences. Both examples demonstrate how AI can significantly enhance customer experience while also driving business growth.

10..2. Subsection 4.2: Personalized Marketing

AI-driven personalized marketing campaigns can help build stronger connections with customers and increase brand loyalty. Stitch Fix, an online personal styling service, leverages AI algorithms to analyse customer preferences, style profiles, and feedback, curating personalized clothing selections for everyone.

10..3. Subsection 4.3: E-commerce and Inventory Management

AI has played a crucial role in helping businesses transition to e-commerce, especially during the COVID-19 pandemic. Using natural language processing and autocomplete suggestions, AI can translate customer searches to deliver the desired products and services. Intelligent product recommendations use data from a customer's browsing habits, searches, and previous purchases to offer suggestions, enhancing the shopping experience.

Section 5: Practical AI Applications in Specific Small Business Scenarios

10..1. Subsection 5.1: Inventory Management for a Family-Owned Takeaway Outlet

A small family-owned takeaway outlet can leverage AI to optimize its inventory management. By analysing sales data, the outlet can identify top-selling food and beverages and the specific days they are most purchased. This data-driven approach can help in forecasting demand, ensuring that popular items are always in stock while reducing wastage from unsold perishables. For instance, a takeaway outlet in New York used AI analytics to discover that their vegan options were selling out faster on Mondays, coinciding with the "Meatless Monday" trend. By preparing more vegan dishes on Mondays and promoting them, they were able to boost sales and customer satisfaction[4].

10..2. Subsection 5.2: Stock Management for a T-Shirt Shop Using Computer Vision

A shop selling t-shirts can employ AI-powered computer vision to streamline its stock management. With cameras and AI algorithms, the system can scan shelves to detect which products are running low or are out of stock. This real-time monitoring eliminates the need for manual stock-taking, ensuring that popular designs and sizes are always available for customers. Furthermore, computer vision can assist in theft prevention. If a t-shirt is removed from the shelf and not paid for, the system can alert the staff, adding an extra layer of security. A boutique t-shirt store in San Francisco implemented an AI-driven computer vision system, which not only helped them keep their inventory up to date but also identified patterns in customer preferences. For instance, the system detected that graphic tees with vintage designs were frequently picked up and examined by customers, especially during the summer months. Leveraging this insight, the store introduced more vintage designs, leading to increased sales.

Author's Insights

In today's dynamic landscape, off-the-shelf software solutions like video creation and text-to-speech tools are empowering SMBs to focus on strategic growth rather than just daily operations. An illustrative example is a modest, family-run bakery I came across that has integrated AI algorithms into its operations. Through AI-driven demand forecasting, the bakery has successfully reduced waste and guaranteed the freshness of its products. This instance underscores how readily available technologies empower small and medium-sized businesses to not only operate 'in' their businesses but also strategically work 'on' them, thereby transforming even conventional industries.

Recommendations

1. **Invest in AI Education**: SMBs should invest in AI education and training programs for their employees. This will help in overcoming the skills gap and make the AI implementation process smoother.

2. **Data Security Measures**: Given the data privacy concerns, SMBs should also invest in robust data security measures to protect customer data.

3. **Consult AI Experts**: It's advisable for SMBs to consult with AI experts or hire a consultant for the initial stages of AI implementation. This will help in choosing the right AI tools that align with the business goals.

Checklist for Pinpointing AI Opportunities within Your Business (Appendix)

This checklist can be used as a guide for SMBs to systematically identify and harness AI opportunities that align with their business goals and lead to meaningful improvements in efficiency and effectiveness. The checklist covers areas such as business analysis, data assessment, technology readiness, skillset evaluation, alignment with business goals, stakeholder engagement, risk assessment, project planning and management, monitoring and evaluation, and continuous improvement.

Conclusion

AI can substantially affect the SME business environment, enhancing efficiency, reducing red tape, securing digital infrastructure, improving access to finance, easing skills management and job matching, and reducing the costs of experimentation. However, to fully reap these benefits, SMBs need to overcome the challenges associated with AI implementation and develop a clear and effective AI strategy. With the right approach and support, SMBs can harness the power of AI to drive growth and innovation. That concludes our chapter and Part two of the book. In the next part of the book Part three we will cover advanced AI Concepts and management. Starting with Chapter 11 The Power of Explainable AI (XAI).

Footnotes

1. " Leveraging AI in Small and Medium Businesses (SMBs): Driving Growth Innovation " https://aiireland.ie/2023/08/30/leveraging-ai-in-small-and-medium-businesses-smbs-driving-growth-and-innovation/

2. " How Artificial Intelligence is helping today´s small Businesses " https://www.forbes.com/sites/charlesrtaylor/2023/08/09/how-artificial-intelligence-is-helping-todays-small-businesses/

3. " Constant Contact Research Reveals Small Businesses Who Use AI Are More Likely to Save Money and be Successful " https://news.constantcontact.com/2023-08-09-Constant-Contact-Research-Reveals-Small-Businesses-Who-Use-AI-Are-More-Likely-to-Save-Money-and-be-Successful

4. AI Ireland interviews 2018-2023 various+

PART 3

AI Concepts and Management

11. Chapter 11:

The Power of Explainable AI (XAI)

Key Takeaways:

1. Trust through Transparency: XAI bridges the gap between complex AI decisions and human understanding, fostering trust in AI-driven outcomes.

2. Broad Applications with Deep Impact: From healthcare to finance, XAI's transparent decision-making is revolutionizing industries, ensuring fairness and clarity.

3. Future-Forward: As AI continues to permeate our world, XAI will be integral, ensuring AI's reasoning remains accessible and accountable.

Introduction: The Imperative of Transparency

In a time when AI decisions can significantly impact outcomes, the lack of transparency around these decisions becomes a pressing concern. This drives us to the critical importance of Explainable AI, as clarity and trust become paramount in today's digital landscape.

The Essence of Explainable AI

XAI isn't just about demystifying AI decisions; it's about fostering trust. As AI systems increasingly influence sectors from finance to healthcare, the need for clear, understandable AI logic becomes paramount.

The Broad Spectrum of XAI Applications

The relevance of XAI is vast and varied:

- **Healthcare:** In the medical field, the stakes are incredibly high. While AI can assist in diagnostics and treatment plans, the "black box" nature of AI algorithms can be a concern. XAI comes into play by offering transparency in AI-driven medical recommendations. It allows medical professionals to understand the reasoning behind an AI's suggestion, thereby acting as a transparent second opinion. This can be crucial for patient trust and for clinicians to make informed decisions.
- **Finance:** The financial sector is increasingly relying on automated systems for trading, risk assessment, and even customer service. In such a landscape, the decisions made by AI have far-reaching implications. XAI provides the much-needed transparency by explaining the logic behind crucial financial decisions. This ensures that individuals and stakeholders are not left in the dark, fostering trust and compliance.
- **Criminal Justice:** AI is being used for predictive policing, parole decisions, and even in judicial sentencing. The risk of bias or error in these systems is a significant concern. XAI can mitigate this by making the AI's decision-making process transparent. This ensures

that any legal decisions assisted by AI can be scrutinized for fairness and ethical considerations, thereby upholding the integrity of the legal system.

The relevance of XAI is not just in making AI understandable but also in building trust and ethical compliance across various sectors.

Pillars of XAI

Two fundamental principles underpin XAI:

- **Interpretability:** It's about ensuring AI's logic is as accessible as a well-articulated narrative.

- **Transparency:** This is the commitment to complete openness about how AI models operate and decide.

Tools and Techniques

- **LIME (Local Interpretable Model-agnostic Explanations):** LIME is a key tool in the XAI toolkit. It works by approximating the complex model with a simpler one that is understandable to humans, but only in a local region around the prediction. This provides localized insights into specific decision points made by the AI. By breaking down complex decisions into simpler, understandable parts, LIME makes the "black box" nature of AI more transparent.
- **Traceability:** Traceability is not just a tool but a fundamental principle in XAI. It ensures that every decision made by an AI system can be traced back to its data sources or the factors that influenced the decision. This is crucial for accountability and for

understanding how a particular output was arrived at. In sectors like healthcare and finance, where decisions have significant consequences, traceability can be indispensable.

Both LIME and Traceability serve to demystify AI decisions, thereby fostering trust and enabling more widespread adoption of AI across various sectors.

Challenges on the Horizon

XAI's journey isn't without hurdles:

- **Complexity vs. Clarity:** One of the most significant challenges in XAI is finding the right balance between providing a detailed, accurate explanation and keeping that explanation simple enough for non-experts to understand. Too much complexity can make the explanation incomprehensible to those without a technical background, defeating the purpose of XAI. On the other hand, overly simplified explanations may lack the nuance needed to fully understand an AI's decision-making process.
- **Performance Trade-offs:** Transparency in AI often comes at a cost. The more interpretable a model is, the less complex it can be, potentially reducing its predictive power. This is a critical consideration, especially in fields like healthcare and finance, where the predictive accuracy of AI can have significant implications. The challenge lies in ensuring sufficient transparency without compromising the AI's effectiveness.

These challenges underscore the intricate path that XAI must navigate to become a standard practice across industries. The goal is to make AI not just powerful, but also transparent and trustworthy.

Expert Insights

The transformative potential of Explainable AI (XAI) is increasingly acknowledged by industry leaders, a fact I witnessed firsthand at the 2022 AI Ireland Awards. Eoin Delaney, who clinched the Young AI Role Model award, stands as a testament to this trend. Based at Insight at UCD, Delaney specializes in counterfactual explanations and case-based reasoning within the XAI domain[1]. His recognition, complemented by multiple best paper awards, serves to highlight the escalating importance of XAI in both scholarly and commercial spheres.

The Future Landscape of XAI

Emerging trends suggest a future where XAI isn't just an add-on but an integral part of AI development. Enhanced tools and methodologies will likely make AI's reasoning even more transparent and accessible.

Author's Personal Insights

In my extensive interviews with AI industry leaders, Explainable AI (XAI) frequently emerges as a focal point. The advantages of XAI are significant. It engenders a level of trust unparalleled by other AI models, which is indispensable in high-stakes sectors like healthcare and finance. Additionally, XAI facilitates a collaborative human-AI interface, aiding in error identification and system improvement. However, it's important to note that XAI is not without its challenges.

The quest for transparency can sometimes compromise the model's predictive accuracy. Moreover, the balance between providing detailed explanations and maintaining simplicity is often hard to strike, which could limit its applicability in certain scenarios. Thus, while XAI is a technological and social imperative, it comes with its own set of complexities that need to be carefully managed[1].

Recommendations

1. **Invest in XAI Research:** Organizations should allocate resources to develop XAI models that align with their specific industry needs.

2. **Educate Stakeholders:** It's crucial to educate both technical and non-technical stakeholders about the benefits and limitations of XAI.

3. **Regular Audits**: Conduct regular audits of AI systems to ensure that they remain explainable and ethical over time.

Case Study: XAI in Healthcare

A recent article highlighted how XAI is revolutionizing the healthcare industry by making AI-driven medical diagnoses transparent. In one instance, XAI was used to explain the AI model's recommendation for a specific cancer treatment, allowing the medical team to understand the rationale behind the decision. This not only built trust but also opened the door for collaborative decision-making between AI and healthcare professionals.

Conclusion: Charting a Transparent Path Forward

As we navigate the intricate maze of an AI-infused future, XAI stands as our compass, ensuring clarity, trust, and collaboration. It's not just about understanding AI but about forging a partnership with it. As we transition into the next chapter, we will delve into dispelling common fears surrounding AI, providing a data-backed perspective on its limitations and capabilities.

Footnotes 1.Eoin Delaney Best Application of AI in a Student Project 2022

https://www.youtube.com/watch?app=desktop&v=7vXnw8wIMsc

12. Chapter 12:

Dispelling AI Fears: A Data-Backed Perspective

Key Takeaways

1. **AI as a Job Evolution Catalyst:** AI doesn't just replace jobs; it creates new, previously unimagined roles.

2. **Collaboration over Competition:** AI is designed to assist, not replace, human judgment and expertise.

3. **AI's Limitation**s: While powerful, AI has its boundaries and operates within the confines of its programming.

Introduction Dispelling AI Fears Through Transparency

As we explored in the previous chapter, Explainable AI (XAI) models can be instrumental in alleviating public fears about AI. For AI to gain widespread trust, it's imperative that organizations prioritize privacy and safety. In this chapter, we examine the dual perceptions of AI as both a utopia and a dystopia. According to a recent survey commissioned by Microsoft, 49% of employees fear job loss due to AI, while 70% believe AI could help manage their increasing workloads[1]. This paradoxical view encapsulates AI's current societal standing—seen as both a liberator from mundane tasks and a potential job eliminator. For business owners and solopreneurs, understanding these perceptions is crucial. It's not just about leveraging AI in your operations but also about preparing your workforce for the changes AI will bring, both positive and negative.

Unravelling the Job Loss Myth

The popular narrative that robots will 'take over' jobs is more complex than it appears. Conversations with industry leaders like Jeff Maggioncalda, CEO of Coursera, and Saadia Zahidi, MD at the World Economic Forum, underscore that technology is transforming tasks rather than just eliminating jobs. The focus is on job evolution, giving rise to new roles that necessitate a synergy between human and machine capabilities. However, it's essential to acknowledge differing viewpoints. Goldman Sachs Research indicates that up to 300 million jobs could be lost to AI[2], highlighting the ongoing debate on this issue. Therefore, while the future may not be as bleak as some predict, caution and preparation are still warranted.

The Dawn of New Professions

AI is not merely a tool for automation; it's an agent of augmentation. It has catalysed the creation of entirely new professions, such as AI ethicists and data privacy managers, that were inconceivable just a decade ago. This evolution in the job market indicates a move towards specialized roles capable of leveraging AI's capabilities for ethical and impactful applications.

AI as a Collaborator, Not Competitor

The true potential of AI lies in its ability to work alongside humans. In healthcare, AI-assisted surgeries have not only reduced errors but have also enabled complex procedures that were previously deemed high-risk. In finance, while robot-advisors manage assets, they rely on human experts for strategy and decision-making. The collaboration between AI and humans is not just beneficial but essential for leveraging the full potential of AI in various sectors.

Author's Insights

During an AI conference in Las Vegas in May 2023, I observed a compelling example of AI-human collaboration at Starbucks. Customer agents used AI to instantly identify negative comments on social media, summarise the concerns, generate an email template, and credit $15 to the customer's account—all within seconds[3]. This showcases the transformative power of AI in enhancing customer service. It's worth noting that the rapid progress in AI has not gone unnoticed by regulatory bodies. Governments and institutions are formulating guidelines to ensure ethical AI usage. The ethical and governance dimensions of AI will be explored in-depth in Chapters 17 and 18, where we will discuss the forthcoming AI Act in Europe. This proactive regulatory stance aims to ensure that AI serves as a catalyst for human progress rather than a societal risk.

Recommendations for the Reader

1. Stay Informed: Keep abreast of the latest developments in AI, especially in your industry. This will help you adapt to changes and possibly identify new career opportunities.

2. Upskill: Consider learning more about AI and related technologies. Many jobs of the future will require a basic understanding of AI principles.

3. **Engage in Dialogue**: Participate in discussions about the ethical and societal implications of AI. Your voice matters in shaping a future where AI benefits everyone.

Conclusion

The path forward with AI is a collaborative and evolving one. As we navigate the future, equipping ourselves with the right knowledge is crucial for a seamless, ethical, and mutually beneficial integration of AI. In the upcoming Chapter 13, we will focus on identifying when external AI expertise is necessary for your business.

Footnotes

1. Will AI Fix Work Microsoft Survey May 9 2023. https://www.microsoft.com/en-us/worklab/work-trend-index/will-ai-fix-work?ranMID=24542&ranEAID=TnL5HPStwNw&ranSiteID=TnL5HPStwNw-fFceTdG1z4M.Hc7n0_UjqA&epi=TnL5HPStwNw-fFceTdG1z4M.Hc7n0_UjqA&irgwc=1&OCID=AIDcmm549zy227_aff_7593_1243925&tduid=%28ir__dtcdgv2vawkfdm9lcwg9sje1bn2xbzdfb9ufhodh00%29%287593%29%281243925%29%28TnL5HPStwNw-fFceTdG1z4M.Hc7n0_UjqA%29%28%29&irclickid=_dtcdgv2vawkfdm9lcwg9sje1bn2xbzdfb9ufhodh00

2. Generative AI Could raise global GDP by 7%

https://www.goldmansachs.com/intelligence/pages/generative-ai-could-raise-global-gdp-by-7-percent.html

3.ServiceNow shows how gen AI could rescue your Starbucks order
https://360magazine.com/2023/05/17/servicenow-starbucks-gen-ai/

13. Chapter 13:

Recognizing the Need for External AI Expertise

Key Takeaways

1. Strategic AI Collaboration: Partnering with external AI expertise can be a game-changer for your organization's growth trajectory.

2. **Evaluation is Key:** A thorough assessment process is vital for ensuring successful AI integration that aligns with your business goals.

3. **Ongoing Engagement:** Building a relationship with your AI vendor is not a one-time task but requires consistent communication and alignment.

Introduction: AI - A Collaborative Endeavor

In the preceding chapter, we delved into dispelling fears surrounding AI adoption. Building on that foundation, this chapter aims to guide you through the critical process of collaborating with external AI experts to maximize your organization's growth and innovation. In the rapidly evolving world of AI, making the right choices can set your organization on a path to success.

Section 1: When to Seek External AI Expertise

Understanding the AI World

The AI field is big and always changing. New tools and methods come out all the time. It's hard for companies to keep up. Knowing when to get help from outside experts can make the difference between just using AI and really making the most of it.

Weighing Up Costs and Benefits

It's important to know what getting outside help will cost you and what you'll get back. A simple cost-benefit analysis can show you the long-term gains compared to the initial spend.

Rules and Regulations

AI has a lot of rules that can be hard to understand. Outside experts can guide you through the legal bits and help you manage risks. This makes sure your AI projects are both legal and ethical.

Section 2: Identifying the Ideal AI Partner

Purpose-Driven Solutions: AI is not a one-size-fits-all solution. Your chosen AI tool should be tailored to address your unique business challenges, ensuring it aligns with your organizational goals.

Ethical Considerations: Ensure that the AI partner you choose aligns with your organization's ethical standards, particularly concerning data privacy and AI ethics.

Checklist for Evaluation:

1. Technical capabilities

2. Ethical alignment

3. Financial stability

4. Industry experience

AI Checklist choosing an AI Vendor

In the appendix is a scoring system to weigh different factors when evaluating potential partners.

Section 3: Cultivating a Productive AI Partnership

Creating a fruitful partnership with an AI expert or firm is more than just signing a contract; it's about establishing a collaborative relationship that adds value to both parties. Here are some key areas to focus on to ensure that the partnership is not only effective but also sustainable:

Shared Vision: A successful partnership is built on mutual understanding and alignment. Clearly define your organization's objectives and ensure they resonate with your AI partner's offerings.

Communication Strategies: Effective communication is key to a successful partnership. Regular updates, meetings, and transparent discussions can foster a healthy relationship.

Conflict Resolution: Addressing conflicts promptly and constructively is crucial. Having a conflict resolution mechanism in place can help maintain a harmonious partnership.

Section 4: Assessing Potential AI Vendors

Selecting an AI partner is a pivotal move. A structured evaluation process ensures you weigh all key aspects, leading to an informed decision.

Vendor Q&A

Compile a list of questions to pose to prospective suppliers. These queries will help you assess their fit for your specific requirements:

1. **Technical Skills:** What are your main AI technical strengths, and how do they match our business needs?
2. **Success Stories:** Can you share case studies where you've successfully implemented AI in similar organisations?
3. **Data Safeguards:** What protocols do you have to ensure data security and regulatory compliance?
4. **Scalability:** How adaptable is your AI solution to our potential growth?
5. **Customer Care:** What level of support can we expect during and after the roll-out?
6. **Ethical Stance:** How do you address ethical issues like AI bias and transparency?
7. **Financial Health:** Can you offer financial records or references confirming your firm's stability and long-term prospects?

Trial Runs

Think about initiating a pilot scheme with a potential supplier to test compatibility and effectiveness before entering a long-term agreement.

Case Study: Transforming Vendor Interaction Through Consultancy Expertise

A leading consultancy firm collaborated with a major IT services company to enhance its vendor interaction experience using AI. This partnership successfully navigated the complexities of vendor management by leveraging advanced AI technologies. The case study underscores the significant impact of external expertise on operational efficiencies and stakeholder interactions. It also highlights the critical role of due diligence and a structured evaluation process in selecting the right consultancy partner for AI implementation.

Author's Insights

Choosing the Right Consultancy: Through my comprehensive interviews with leaders from over 200 consultancy firms, including industry stalwarts like Boston Consulting Group and Accenture, the recurring theme has been the critical importance of selecting the right consultancy partner at the right time in your AI journey. A standout discussion with Liam McKenna from Mazars underscored the necessity of delivering successful data science projects while adhering to data privacy norms[1].

The Importance of Teamwork: While the spotlight often falls on technology in AI discussions, the human element is equally crucial. A successful AI initiative is not solely about algorithms and data; it's about the collective efforts of the people involved.

Data as a Decision-Making Tool: My interviews have consistently stressed the pivotal role of data analytics in making well-informed decisions. Effective data utilisation can offer invaluable insights into the compatibility and efficacy of a prospective AI partnership.

Ethical Imperatives: Ethical compatibility between your organisation and your AI partner is more than just a compliance requirement; it's a foundational element for enduring success. My dialogues with industry leaders have repeatedly emphasised the significance of ethical considerations in AI, ranging from data privacy to algorithmic fairness.

Recommendations

1. **Due Diligence:** Never underestimate the importance of due diligence. Beyond technical capabilities, investigate a potential partner's financial stability, ethical standing, and industry reputation.

2. **Pilot Testing**: Before fully committing to a partnership, consider a pilot phase to test the waters. This allows for adjustments and fine-tuning before a full-scale implementation.

3. **Post-Implementation Review**: After the AI system is integrated, conduct a post-implementation review to assess the ROI and overall success of the partnership.

Conclusion

Setting out on the AI journey is both exhilarating and demanding. With this guide in hand, organisations are well-equipped to navigate the complexities of AI partnerships, optimising the advantages of AI whilst fostering a harmonious relationship with their selected AI specialist. As we turn our attention to the forthcoming chapter, we will delve into the nuances of AI Project Management, a vital component that guarantees the successful deployment and expansion of your AI endeavours.

Footnotes

Liam McKenna Mazars Interview AI Ireland Podcast
https://aiireland.ie/2019/11/14/e51-liam-mckenna-mazars-ireland/

14. Chapter 14:

AI in Project Management - Unleashing the Power of AI

Key Takeaways

1. AI enhances project execution, decision-making, and alignment with strategic goals [1].

2. Gartner's prediction is that by 2030 AI could result in the elimination of about 80% of routine work in project management [2].

3. 62% of experts stress the importance of acquiring new skills for effective AI utilization[3].

Introduction

Building on Chapter 13, which emphasizes the importance of having the right AI expertise onboard, this chapter delves into the transformative role of AI in Project Management. With only 35% of projects completing successfully [4], the need for innovative solutions is paramount. This chapter incorporates insights from a recent survey conducted in August 2023.

The AI-Powered Evolution of Project Management:

AI's integration into project management is a paradigm shift that goes beyond task automation. Predictive analytics and intelligent task allocation provided by AI significantly reduce administrative burdens.

According to Harvard Business Review, machine learning can detect patterns that humans can't, leading to more accurate predictions[5].

Streamlining Administrative Efficiency:

AI serves as a catalyst for operational efficiency by automating routine tasks, thereby liberating managerial staff to concentrate on activities of greater strategic importance[6]. The advent of AI-driven chatbots and virtual assistants has been a game-changer in the realm of communication and task management. These intelligent tools not only automate day-to-day communications but also empower project managers to dedicate their time more effectively to strategic planning and critical decision-making[7].

Reshaping Project Scope and Leadership with AI:

AI's predictive capabilities empower leaders to anticipate risks, adjust resources dynamically, and ensure alignment with organizational goals. According to Gartner's research, by 2030, 80% of project management tasks will be run by AI, powered by big data and machine learning[2].

AI in Action: Real-World Use Cases:

The transformative power of AI is not merely theoretical; it manifests in practical applications that have a direct impact on business operations. Key areas where AI has proven its mettle include Task Decomposition, Predictive Analytics, and Intelligent Resource Allocation.

- **Task Decomposition:** AI algorithms can break down complex projects into manageable tasks, prioritising them based on various factors such as urgency, resource availability, and strategic importance. This enables more efficient project management and execution.

- **Predictive Analytics:** AI-driven analytics tools can forecast trends, customer behaviours, and potential bottlenecks, allowing businesses to make data-backed decisions that enhance performance and profitability.

- **Intelligent Resource Allocation:** AI systems can dynamically allocate resources based on real-time data, ensuring optimal utilisation and reducing waste. This is particularly beneficial in industries where resource management is critical, such as manufacturing and logistics.

These real-world use cases underscore the practical benefits of integrating AI into business operations, offering not just efficiency but also a competitive edge.

Swift and Efficient Integration:

One of the standout advantages of AI is its ability to bring speed and efficiency to business operations. By automating manual processes and facilitating task decomposition, AI enables organisations to execute projects more swiftly and allocate resources more judiciously. This rapid integration of AI capabilities into existing workflows not only streamlines operations but also provides a significant competitive advantage[1].

Insights from the "Unleashing the Power of Artificial Intelligence in Project Management" Survey:

This section elaborates on the extensive survey conducted by Prof. Antonio Nieto-Rodriguez and Prof. Ricardo Viana Vargas, Ph.D. Drawing from the expertise of 772 professionals across 95 countries, the survey provides a nuanced understanding of AI's transformative role in project management[8]. Not only does it affirm AI's capacity to enhance project execution, decision-making, and strategic alignment, but it also stresses the immediate need for skill adaptation in emerging areas like data analytics and AI tool management.

The survey reveals a heightened awareness of ethical considerations, with 74.78% of experts voicing concerns about the ethical implications of AI-based decision-making. It also identifies AI as a catalyst for innovation, endorsed by 65.13% of respondents, and underscores the industry's willingness to invest in AI exploration, with over 50% being very likely to invest[8].

However, the survey doesn't shy away from outlining the challenges and barriers in AI integration. It calls for strategic planning and meticulous implementation to overcome these hurdles. This multi-dimensional perspective offers a balanced view, acknowledging both the promise and the complexities of integrating AI into project management.

Author's Insights

In my extensive interviews with AI leaders from companies like Google and IBM, there's a consensus: AI is transformative in project management. This is backed by Prof. Antonio Nieto-Rodriguez's survey, where 74.79% of experts affirm AI's role in enhancing project execution and decision-making. Strategic adoption is key. The survey reveals that 62% of experts stress the need for new skills to effectively use AI. It's not just a plug-and-play solution; it's a strategic asset, a point supported by 41.06% of experts who noted improvements in project delivery with AI tools[8].

Ethical considerations are crucial. The survey indicates that 74.78% of experts have ethical concerns about AI in decision-making. This underscores the need for robust ethical frameworks to build trust with stakeholders[8].

Recommendations

1. **Invest in AI Training Programs:** Consider programs to equip your team with the necessary skills.
2. **Collaborate with AI Experts:** Establish partnerships with AI firms or consultants to ensure successful integration.
3. **Ethical Guidelines:** Develop a set of ethical guidelines for AI utilization in project management.

Future Outlook

As AI technologies continue to evolve, we can expect more sophisticated tools and algorithms that will further revolutionize project management.

Conclusion

The integration of AI into project management isn't a future concept; it's a present reality. As AI's role evolves, its influence on shaping project management's future becomes even more pronounced. For executives, understanding and harnessing AI-driven tools and strategies is imperative for project success and organizational growth. However, it's crucial to acknowledge that the journey to AI integration is not without its challenges.

As we transition into the next chapter, we will delve into a critical aspect that every executive should be aware of the risks associated with AI projects and how to mitigate them. Chapter 15, "Overcoming AI Project Failures: Risks and Remedies," will provide you with the insights and strategies to navigate the complexities and challenges that come with implementing AI in your projects.

Footnotes

1. "How AI Transforms Project Management "
https://www.linkedin.com/pulse/how-ai-transforms-project-management-giovanni-sisinna#:~:text=In%20summary%2C%20AI%20transforms%20project,leaders%20can%20radically%20enhance%20outcomes.

2. Artificial Intelligence in Project Management: What impact will AI Have. AI In Project Management

3. "New Research: Over Half of Workers Say Generative AI Will Help Advance Their Career, but Most Lack the Skills "
https://www.salesforce.com/news/stories/generative-ai-skills-research/

4. "How AI Transforms Project Management"
https://hbr.org/2023/02/how-ai-will-transform-project-

management#:~:text=Project%20Management%20Today%20and%20Path%20Forward&text=Yet%20according%20to%20the%20Standish,the%20modernization%20of%20project%20management.

5. " How to win with Machine Learning "

https://hbr.org/2020/09/how-to-win-with-machine-learning#:~:text=Making%20Predictions%20with%20AI,help%20make%20a%20product%20better.

6. " Pioneering AI In Work Management "

https://www.wrike.com/blog/pioneering-ai-work-management/#:~:text=Intelligent%20automation%3A%20Wrike's%20AI%20algorithms,%2C%20problem%20solving%2C%20and%20creativity.

7. " Project Management AI: What is it? "

https://www.process.st/project-management-ai/#:~:text=Artificial%20Intelligence%2DPowered%20Assistants&text=These%20assistants%20use%20machine%20learning,critical%20decision%2Dmaking%20and%20execution

8. AI-Driven Project Management Revolution Survey Findings by Prof. Antonio Nieto-Rodriguez Prof. Ricardo Viana Vargas, PhD

https://antonionietorodriguez.com/pmairevolution/

15. Chapter 15

Overcoming AI Project Failures: Risks and Remedies

Key Takeaways

1. Empirical Insights Matter: The importance of empirical data and expert opinions cannot be overstated when it comes to understanding the critical factors that lead to AI project failures.

2. Balancing Act: A successful AI project requires a delicate balance between organizational and technological challenges. Failing to address either can lead to project termination.

3. Lessons from Real-world Events: The COVID-19 pandemic revealed significant gaps in AI's capabilities, especially in healthcare. These lessons serve as a cautionary tale for future AI implementations.

Introduction

As we continue to explore the multifaceted world of Artificial Intelligence (AI) in business, it's crucial to address a topic that often goes unspoken: the failure of AI projects. While the previous chapter focused on the positive impact of AI in project management, this chapter aims to delve into the complexities and challenges that often lead to the downfall of AI initiatives. By understanding these pitfalls, organizations can better prepare themselves for the AI journey ahead, maximizing the chances of success while minimizing risks. This chapter will provide empirical insights, discuss the balance between organizational and technological challenges, and share lessons from real-world events to offer a comprehensive guide on overcoming AI project failures.

The Reality of AI Project Failures

While AI promises transformative benefits, many firms find themselves unable to harness its full potential. A study reveals that while challenges in AI projects are well-documented, the critical factors leading to project failure remain largely unknown. The allure of AI often leads organizations to jump in without a full understanding of the complexities involved. This lack of preparedness can result in projects that are either terminated prematurely or fail to deliver the expected outcomes. It's not just about having the right technology; it's also about having a clear roadmap, measurable objectives, and an understanding of the potential pitfalls. The absence of these elements often leads to project failures, costing companies time, resources, and credibility.

Organizational and Technological Challenges

AI project failures can be attributed to a mix of organizational and technological issues. Organizational challenges may include a lack of clear strategy, inadequate stakeholder buy-in, or insufficient training. On the technological front, issues like data quality, integration complexities, or unsuitable algorithms can derail projects. It's crucial to understand that these challenges are often interlinked. For example, poor data quality may be a result of inadequate stakeholder buy-in, leading to insufficient resources being allocated for data cleansing. Similarly, a lack of clear strategy can result in the selection of unsuitable algorithms, causing the project to fail. Addressing these challenges requires a holistic approach that considers both organizational readiness and technological capabilities.

Unearthing the Critical Factors

To truly understand the reasons behind AI project failures, it's essential to delve deeper into their critical factors. Interviews with AI experts across various industries have shed light on both known and previously unidentified factors that can lead to project termination. These interviews reveal that the landscape of AI project failures is far more nuanced than commonly understood. Factors such as misaligned business objectives, unrealistic expectations, and poor communication often contribute to project failures but are seldom discussed in mainstream conversations about AI.

Moreover, the experts point out that the failure of an AI project is rarely due to a single issue. It is often a cascade of challenges, each exacerbating the other, leading to the eventual termination of the project. For instance, poor data quality could lead to ineffective algorithms, which in turn could result in failed objectives and loss of stakeholder trust. This multi-faceted nature of AI project failures underscores the need for a comprehensive, multi-disciplinary approach to project management. Organizations need to be vigilant at every step, from initial planning and stakeholder engagement to the final deployment and post-implementation review, to mitigate the risks effectively.

Empirical Insights: Understanding the Critical Factors

The article published in Procedia Computer Science provides empirical data on the critical factors that lead to the failure of AI projects[1]. Conducted through interviews with experts in the AI field across different industries, the study identifies both organizational and technological issues as key contributors to project failure.

Organizational vs Technological Issues: Balancing between organizational and technological challenges is essential for the success of an AI project.

Expert Interviews: The weight given to expert opinions can be invaluable when assessing the risks and remedies for AI project failures.

Empirical Data: The new empirical data presented in the article can be used to develop a more robust framework for AI project management.

Lessons from the Pandemic: Where AI Fell Short

The COVID-19 pandemic tested AI's capabilities, especially in healthcare, revealing significant shortcomings[2]. Four key areas were identified: bad datasets, automated discrimination, human failures, and a complex global context.

Bad datasets hindered AI's accuracy, exacerbated by the urgency of healthcare decisions. Automated discrimination, fuelled by biased data, raised ethical concerns. Human errors, such as misinterpreting AI data, compounded these issues. Lastly, the multi-dimensional nature of the pandemic—spanning healthcare, social, and economic sectors—proved too complex for existing AI systems to navigate effectively. The pandemic serves as a cautionary tale, emphasizing the need for more robust, ethical, and adaptable AI solutions.

Moving Forward: Remedies and Best Practices

To navigate the complexities and pitfalls of AI projects, organizations must adopt a multi-faceted approach that addresses both organizational and technological challenges.

15.1 Below are some key strategies:

15.1.1 Stakeholder Engagement: One of the primary reasons AI projects fails is a lack of alignment among stakeholders. It's crucial to ensure that everyone involved—from executives to data scientists—understands the project's goals, timelines, and limitations. Regular communication and updates can help maintain this alignment and prevent misunderstandings that could derail the project.

15.1.2 Robust Data Strategy: Data is the lifeblood of any AI project. However, poor data quality can lead to ineffective algorithms and, ultimately, project failure. Organizations should prioritize data quality and integration, ensuring that the AI models are trained on accurate, comprehensive datasets. This involves not just technical solutions but also governance policies to manage data effectively.

15.1.3 Continuous Learning: The fast-paced nature of AI technology means that what works today may not be effective tomorrow. Organizations should foster a culture of continuous learning and adaptation. This involves regular training sessions, staying updated on the latest AI research, and being willing to pivot strategies when faced with challenges or new information.

The Role of Culture in AI Project Failures

Organizational culture plays a pivotal role in the success or failure of AI projects. A culture that fosters innovation, encourages risk-taking, and values data-driven decision-making is more likely to successfully implement AI initiatives. Conversely, a culture resistant to change or one that does not prioritize data can be a significant roadblock.

15.2.1 Cultural Resistance: One of the most common cultural issues is resistance to the changes that AI brings. This resistance can manifest in various forms, from skepticism about AI's capabilities to fear of job displacement. Overcoming this resistance requires strong leadership and clear communication about the benefits of AI, not just for the organization but also for individual employees.

15.2.2 Data Culture: A culture that does not value data will struggle with AI projects. Data is the foundation upon which AI is built, and an organization that does not understand its importance will face challenges in data quality, integration, and governance.

15.2.3 Agility and Adaptability: The fast-paced evolution of AI technologies requires a culture that can adapt quickly. Organizations that are set in their ways and slow to adapt to new technologies and methodologies are less likely to succeed in their AI initiatives.

15.2.4 Leadership's Role: Leadership plays a crucial role in shaping organizational culture. Effective leaders can drive cultural change by setting a vision, aligning AI projects with business objectives, and fostering an environment where learning and adaptation are encouraged.

Author's Insights

The Human Element: While technology is at the core of AI projects, the human element cannot be ignored. From stakeholder alignment to ethical considerations, the success of an AI project often hinges on human decisions and actions.

Data Governance: My interviews with industry leaders have emphasized the importance of robust data governance policies. Ensuring data quality and ethical usage is not just a technical requirement but a business imperative.

Interdisciplinary Approach: AI is not just a technological endeavour but an interdisciplinary one. It requires the collaboration of data scientists, domain experts, ethicists, and business leaders to be truly effective.

Case Studies

Healthcare example: In one of my interviews with the CTO of Healthcare provider, a company specializing in AI-driven diagnostics, a compelling story unfolded. The company launched an AI model designed to diagnose a specific type of cancer at its early stages. Despite the model's high accuracy in lab tests, it failed in the real-world applications. Upon investigation, it was discovered that the training data was skewed towards patients from a particular geographic region, making the model less effective for a diverse patient population. This case is an example of the importance of diverse and representative data sets in AI projects[3].

Future Outlook

As AI continues to evolve, so too will the challenges and opportunities it presents. Organizations must be agile and adaptive to navigate this ever-changing landscape.

Conclusion

AI projects hold immense potential, but they also come with their set of challenges. By understanding and addressing the critical factors behind project failures, organizations can better position themselves for AI success. The empirical insights and expert opinions offer a robust framework for navigating both organizational and technological challenges. Moreover, real-world events like the COVID-19 pandemic serve as cautionary tales, highlighting the need for a comprehensive strategy that includes data quality, stakeholder engagement, and continuous learning[2]. As we move forward, it becomes increasingly clear that mastering AI is not just about the technology but also about the people who make it work. This brings us to the focus of our next chapter, Chapter 16: Mastering AI Skills and Talent Acquisition. In this upcoming chapter, we will delve into the importance of skills and talent as part of a combined strategy for AI success. The right talent can serve as the linchpin that holds the complex machinery of AI projects together, ensuring not just implementation but also long-term sustainability.

Footnotes

1. Failure of AI Projects: understanding the critical factors by Jens Westenberger & Kajetan Schuler Procedia Computer Science
Failure of AI projects: understanding the critical factors
2. Why AI failed to live Up to its potential during the pandemic by Bhaskar Chakravorti March 2022 Why AI Failed to Live UP HBR
3. AI Ireland Interviews various 2018-2023

16. Chapter 16:

Mastering AI Skills and Talent Acquisition

Key Takeaways:

1. AI is revolutionizing the business landscape, making the acquisition of the right talent crucial for success.

2. Building an AI-proficient team requires a blend of technical, business, and ethical skills.

3. Leadership plays a pivotal role in fostering a culture of continuous learning and AI integration[1].

Introduction

In Chapter 14, we discussed AI Project Management, and in Chapter 15, we explored overcoming AI project failures. Now, in Chapter 16, we delve into Mastering AI Skills and Talent Acquisition. As the Co-Founder and Chief Customer Officer of a specialist international AI Staffing firm, I bring considerable first-hand experience of knowledge to this topic.

This chapter aims to provide strategies and insights to help organizations navigate the complex landscape of AI talent acquisition and build a robust, AI-adept team. I recall a conversation with a CEO of a burgeoning tech start-up who was initially overwhelmed by the rapid advancements in AI[2].

However, with the right strategies and talent, his company not only built a robust AI team but also launched an innovative AI-driven product. This transformation underscores the power of the right talent.

Section 1: Navigating the AI Revolution

16..1. Riding the AI Wave

Artificial Intelligence (AI) is not merely a technological trend; it is a transformative force that is fundamentally altering the way businesses operate. From automating complex tasks to extracting actionable insights from vast data sets, AI is a game-changer. According to Gartner, by 2022, as much as 85% of enterprises will have integrated AI into their operations[3]. This integration is not just about implementing AI tools but also about understanding the broader AI ecosystem. Companies need to be aware of the latest advancements, from machine learning algorithms to natural language processing capabilities, and how these can be applied to solve real-world business challenges.

Reflection Point: Consider your organization's current AI utilization. Where do you envision its most impactful application?

Are you looking at AI merely as a tool for automation, or are you exploring its potential to drive innovation and create new business models?

Section 2: Building an AI-Savvy Team

16..1. Attracting New Talent

In the fiercely competitive landscape of AI talent acquisition, what sets you apart is what you offer candidates. Competitive salaries are a given, but top-tier AI professionals are also looking for more. They seek opportunities for professional growth, a chance to work on cutting-edge AI projects, and a culture that fosters innovation. Organizations should also consider offering equity options, especially for start-ups, to attract high-calibre talent. Moreover, the work environment should encourage collaboration and knowledge sharing, as AI is often most effective when it is a cross-disciplinary effort.

16..2. Continuous Training and Development

Retaining AI talent is not just about offering a good salary; it's about creating a conducive environment for continuous learning and growth. Organizations must invest in regular training programs, workshops, and certifications to keep their AI teams updated with the latest advancements. This could range from technical training in new programming languages and AI frameworks to soft skills like project management and effective communication. A culture that values ongoing development not only retains talent but also ensures that the team is always equipped with the latest skills to drive AI initiatives successfully.

Section 3: The AI Skillset

16..1. Technical Skills

Technical skills form the bedrock of AI expertise. This includes not only programming languages like Python, R, and Java but also specialized frameworks and libraries such as TensorFlow, Py Torch, and scikit-learn. Additionally, a deep understanding of algorithms, data structures, and machine learning models is essential. However, the realm of AI extends far beyond these foundational skills. As AI systems become more complex and integrated into various business functions, professionals also need to be proficient in cloud computing, cybersecurity, and data engineering.

16..2. Business Skills

An effective AI professional is not just a technician but a strategist. They must be able to integrate their technical know-how with business insights. This involves understanding the company's strategic goals, the competitive landscape, and how AI can provide a competitive edge. Skills like project management, stakeholder communication, and financial acumen are also crucial. An AI expert should be able to translate complex technical concepts into business language, making it easier for decision-makers to understand the value and impact of AI initiatives.

16..3. Ethical and Legal Skills

The rise of AI has brought with it a host of ethical and legal challenges, from data privacy issues to algorithmic bias. Professionals in the AI field need to be well-versed in these areas to navigate the complexities of AI implementation responsibly. This includes understanding regulations like GDPR for data protection and being aware of the ethical implications of AI, such as its impact on employment and social dynamics.

Section 4: The Role of Leadership

16..1. Cultivating a Learning Culture

Leadership plays a pivotal role in fostering a culture of continuous learning within an organization. This goes beyond merely endorsing skill development programs. Leaders should actively participate in learning initiatives, whether it's taking an AI course or attending industry seminars. By doing so, they not only set the tone for AI integration but also demonstrate a commitment to personal and organizational growth. A learning culture encourages employees to take risks, innovate, and adapt to the rapidly evolving AI landscape.

16..2. Leading by Example

Leaders should be at the forefront of AI adoption, demonstrating a commitment to understanding and leveraging AI's potential. This involves staying updated on AI trends, collaborating with AI experts, and even participating in AI projects. By leading by example, they not only set a positive precedent but also create an environment where employees feel empowered to explore AI technologies.

Author's Insights

I've observed a common thread: the importance of a multi-disciplinary approach to AI talent. It's not just about technical acumen; it's about a holistic skill set that includes business strategy, ethics, and continuous learning. I've seen companies transform their AI capabilities by adopting a more comprehensive approach to talent acquisition and management. This involves not just hiring the right people, but also investing in their continuous development and aligning them with the company's strategic objectives.

Recommendations

Invest in Upskilling: Don't just look for talent outside; invest in upskilling your current workforce.

Diversity in AI: Aim for a diverse team to bring different perspectives and approaches to problem-solving.

Ethical AI: Make ethics a core part of your AI strategy, not an afterthought.

Conclusion

Mastering AI skills and talent acquisition extends far beyond merely recruiting the right individuals. It involves cultivating an ecosystem where AI can flourish, from the leadership echelons down to the frontline staff. By grasping the intricacies of AI talent and nurturing a culture of perpetual learning, organizations can strategically place themselves at the vanguard of the AI revolution.

This chapter marks the conclusion of Part III of the book, which delved into Advanced AI Concepts and Management. We explored a range of topics including the transformative impact of Explainable AI, dispelling common fears surrounding AI, the importance of external AI expertise, effective AI project management, strategies to overcome AI project failures, and, of course, mastering AI skills and talent acquisition.

As we transition into Part IV, we will shift our focus to the ethical and regulatory dimensions of AI. We will commence this section with a deep dive into the key considerations for ethical AI deployment, laying the groundwork for a comprehensive understanding of the moral and legal implications of AI technologies.

Footnotes

1. " Culture of Continuous Learning: Embracing Excellence with a Learning Culture " https://claned.com/culture-of-continuous-learning-embracing-excellence-with-a-learning-culture/#:~:text=Leadership%20Buy%2DIn%3A%20The%20commitment,its%20significance%20to%20the%20workforce

2. AI Ireland Interviews 2018-2023

3. According to Gartner, by 2022, as much as 85% of enterprises will have integrated AI into their operations. 2. AI In Project Management. What Impact will it have? https://corasystems.com/blog/impact-artificial-intelligence-in-project-management/

Part IV

Ethical and Regulatory Considerations

17. Chapter 17:

The Ethical Dimension: Key Considerations in AI Deployment

Key Takeaways

1. **Shared Responsibility:** Everyone in the organization has a role to play in ensuring AI is used ethically.

2. Team Effort: Solving ethical dilemmas in AI isn't just a job for the tech team. It needs input from ethicists, legal experts, and other key players.

3. Stay Updated: The world of AI is always changing. Continuous learning is a must for using AI responsibly.

Introduction

Welcome to the fourth section of this book, which delves into the legal and ethical dimensions of employing AI in the business realm. This specific chapter zeroes in on the ethical implications associated with AI deployment. For business leaders, comprehending the capabilities of AI is insufficient; it's vital to utilize it in a manner that is both efficient and ethically sound.

Section 1: Unlocking AI's Potential

AI has the potential to enhance various business operations, offering transformative benefits. But to harness these benefits, a structured approach is essential.

17..1. 1.1 Guide to Identifying AI Opportunities:

Identiffy Needs: As discussed in Chapter 10. Start by pinpointing the challenges your business faces. Look for areas where AI can improve customer service, streamline operations, or boost product development. This ensures your AI projects align with your business goals.

Assess and Research: Understand AI's capabilities and its relevance to your challenges. Explore case studies and success stories to gauge AI's potential impact on your business.

Quality Data: Data is the fuel for AI. Make sure you have access to high-quality data and think about investing in data management tools. The better the data, the more effective your AI will be.

Cost-Benefit Analysis: Before diving in, weigh the costs against the expected benefits. Look at expenses, time, manpower, and any potential risks. A feasibility study can give you a clear picture of the return on investment.

Test Run: Before going all-in, start with a small-scale pilot project. This minimizes risk and provides valuable insights into how the AI will perform in a real-world setting.

Iterate and Improve: Use the feedback from the pilot phase to fine-tune your AI solution. This ongoing refinement ensures that your AI initiatives stay aligned with your business objectives.

Section 2: The Ethical Compass of AI

Ethical Imperative in Business: As AI becomes integral to business operations, ethical considerations are not just a moral obligation but a business necessity. A 2023 research paper in HRM Review highlights that ethical AI practices can mitigate risks and enhance brand reputation, making it a key concern for business leaders[1].

17..1. Ethical Considerations Checklist for Business Leaders:

Privacy: Protecting data is not just a legal requirement but a business imperative. Complying with data privacy laws safeguards your company's reputation and minimizes legal risks.

Transparency: Openness about how AI is used in your operations builds trust with stakeholders, from employees to customers. This trust is essential for long-term business success and ethical compliance.

Fairness: Using diverse data sets for AI training avoids biases that could harm your brand and lead to legal repercussions. Regular audits can identify and correct these biases.

Accountability: When AI errors occur, having a clear responsibility framework not only helps in quick redressal but also builds stakeholder trust. It's not just the technology that needs to be accountable but also the people using it.

Oversight: Implementing human oversight ensures that AI decisions align with your company's ethical and business standards. It provides a safety net to review and, if needed, override AI decisions.

Section 3: Preparing for the Future of AI

17..1. Continuous Learning for Business-wide concern.

AI is a fast-evolving field. Companies must not only keep up but stay ahead.

This involves ongoing education, which can be facilitated through in-house training, educational partnerships, or online courses and certifications.

17..2. Cross-Functional Collaboration

AI isn't just an IT issue; it's a business-wide concern. Collaboration across departments like marketing, HR, and legal is essential. Regular cross-departmental meetings should focus on the ethical, operational, and strategic aspects of AI initiatives

17..3. Ethical Leadership for Long-Term Success

Leadership in the AI era is about more than just business acumen; it's about ethical foresight. Executives must be fluent in ethical guidelines and ensure these are built into the AI strategy. Openness to external audits can further validate compliance and build trust.

17..4. Staying Ahead of the Regulatory Curve

It's not enough to just know current AI regulations; you must anticipate what's coming. A dedicated team or role should be in place to keep an eye on evolving laws and guidelines.

17..5. Understanding AI's Broader Impact

AI's influence isn't limited to your organization. It can affect job markets, data security, and even democratic systems. Regular assessments of these broader impacts can guide strategy adjustments.

Section 4: Case Study

17..1. Case Study: Navigating Ethical Complexities in AI-Driven Healthcare

Company: Medical Device Company

The Challenge: Leveraging AI to forecast patient outcomes while rigorously maintaining data privacy and ethical standards.

Strategic Approach: A multi-disciplinary team of ethicists and data scientists collaborated to develop an AI model that prioritizes patient confidentiality and minimizes bias. A pilot study was conducted to evaluate both the model's performance and its ethical ramifications.

Results: The AI model demonstrated high predictive accuracy in patient outcomes while fully complying with ethical guidelines. This led to the company earning an ethics certification, thereby enhancing its market credibility[2].

Section 5: The Role of Leadership in AI Integration

17..1. Fostering a Learning Culture

Leaders are instrumental in cultivating an ethos of continuous learning within the organisation. They should allocate resources for employee training and encourage knowledge-sharing sessions, thereby setting the stage for successful AI integration.

17..2. Leading Through Action

Leaders must be proactive in AI adoption, exemplifying a commitment to understanding its capabilities. Active participation in AI projects or educational courses sends a compelling message about the technology's significance.

17..3. Ethical Governance

Ethical leadership extends beyond legal compliance; it sets the moral direction for the organisation. Leaders must be conversant with ethical guidelines related to AI and ensure their incorporation into the company's AI strategy. They should also be amenable to external audits for compliance verification.

17..4. Strategic Foresight

Leaders must possess a coherent vision for integrating AI into the organisation's long-term objectives. This entails a nuanced understanding of the associated risks and benefits, enabling informed decision-making that aligns with organisational values

Recommendations

17..1. Ethical Oversight

It is advisable for organisations to institute an ethical auditing mechanism for their AI systems. Regular evaluations should be conducted to verify that AI algorithms operate as intended and adhere to ethical norms. An external audit can offer an impartial viewpoint and enhance credibility.

17..2. Data Governance

Effective data governance is essential for ethical AI deployment. Organisations should form a data governance committee comprising data scientists, ethicists, and legal professionals. This committee is responsible for overseeing data collection, storage, and usage, ensuring adherence to privacy laws and ethical principles

17..3. Skill Development Initiatives

Investment in skill development programmes is crucial for staying competitive in the fast-paced AI sector. These programmes should encompass both technical and ethical aspects of AI, equipping teams to manage the complexities of AI implementation.

17..4. Stakeholder Involvement

Active engagement with stakeholders, including employees, customers, and the broader community, offers valuable perspectives on the ethical ramifications of AI projects. Methods such as open forums, surveys, and feedback sessions can be employed to gather stakeholder input

17..5. Transparency and Accountability

Transparency in AI operations and accountability for outcomes are vital for ethical AI practices. Organisations should disclose information about their AI algorithms, data sources, and decision-making processes. This fosters trust and enables more informed decisions by all involved parties

17..6. Legal Readiness

In light of the dynamic legal landscape surrounding AI, organisations must be prepared for legal challenges. This involves staying abreast of current laws, retaining legal expertise, and being ready for legal audits.

17..7. Author's Insights

Ethics are integral to AI-focused organisations. This ethical alignment offers competitive advantages in regulatory compliance, talent acquisition, and customer engagement[3]. Dr. Alessandra, an Associate Professor and SFI Funded Investigator, concurs, emphasizing the importance of transparency, trust, and fairness in high-stakes AI decisions[4]. I advocate for structured, multi-stakeholder dialogues to address ethical challenges effectively.

Key Insights from Interviews

Competitive Edge: Ethical AI practices enhance regulatory navigation and attract top talent.

Customer Trust: Ethical conduct in AI fosters customer loyalty.

Regulatory Readiness: Proactive ethical measures reduce regulatory risks.

Conclusion

As we conclude Chapter 17, it's evident that the ethical deployment of AI is a multifaceted challenge requiring a collective, multi-disciplinary approach. This chapter has aimed to provide a comprehensive guide to navigating the complex ethical landscape of AI, emphasizing the importance of responsible deployment. As we transition to Chapter 18, the focus will shift to creating effective AI governance structures. Governance is not merely about compliance; it's about establishing a framework that allows AI to be both innovative and ethical. This will be a natural progression from the ethical considerations discussed in this chapter to the structural mechanisms that ensure these considerations are effectively implemented.

In the upcoming chapters, we will delve deeper into these themes, providing actionable insights and strategies for organizations aiming to lead in the AI era responsibly.

Footnotes

1. An Artificial intelligence algorithmic approach to ethical decision-making in HRM processes by HRM Review – Waymond Rodgers and James Murray
https://www.sciencedirect.com/science/article/pii/S1053482222000432

2. AI Ireland Interviews 2018-2023

3. " Expert Analysis on the Ethical Considerations and Challenges Surrounding AI in the Future. "
https://www.linkedin.com/pulse/expert-analysis-ethical-considerations-challenges-ai-future-phillips#:~:text=Interdisciplinary%20collaboration%20is%20essential%20in,and%20deployment%20of%20AI%20technologies.

4. " AI Ireland Podcast Episode 66"
AI Ireland Podcast Series - Episode 6

18. Chapter 18:

AI Governance and Ethics

Key Takeaways

1. Data Governance: Ensuring data quality, ethical, and secure use.

2. AI Model Management: Overseeing the lifecycle and ethics of AI models.

3. Ethical and Legal Pathways: Navigating the moral and legal dimensions of AI.

Introduction

Building on our discussion in Chapter 17 about "The Ethical Dimension: Key Considerations in AI Deployment," this chapter delves deeper into the governance and ethical frameworks that underpin AI technologies. As AI continues to evolve and integrate into various aspects of business and society, the importance of governance and ethical considerations cannot be overstated.

Data Governance: The Lifeblood of AI

Data is more than just digital information; it's the foundation upon which AI operates. Proper governance ensures that this data is not only accurate but also used ethically and securely. Implications of unethical data use and potential risks associated with data breaches can be significant, affecting both businesses and their customers [1].

AI Model Management: The Evolution of AI

AI models aren't static; they evolve and adapt. Overseeing this journey, from inception to retirement, is essential to ensure they serve their intended purpose effectively. Understanding model limitations and potential biases is crucial for businesses to ensure fair and unbiased AI applications.

Oversight Mechanisms: Guiding the AI Journey

In the vast realm of AI, oversight mechanisms act as our compass, ensuring we remain on the right path. The complexities of AI can sometimes make oversight challenging, necessitating the involvement of experts in the oversight committee.

Author's Insights

The AI field is always changing, offering both opportunities and challenges. Good governance is about more than just following the rules; it's key to using AI in an ethical and responsible way. Many companies are hesitant to start AI projects because they're worried about meeting all the legal requirements. But once they commit to strong governance, things get easier. Starting with a focus on data privacy not only meets legal standards but also builds confidence that the company is acting ethically. By following the guidelines in this chapter, companies can use AI more confidently and ethically.

Data Governance: The Foundation for Ethical AI

Data Governance is not just a technical requirement but a cornerstone for ethical AI. It involves systematic management of data assets to ensure quality, security, and regulatory compliance.

Key Recommendations for Data Governance

- Quality Assurance: Implement regular audits and validation to ensure data accuracy and integrity.
- Privacy Protocols: Utilise encryption and anonymisation methods to protect sensitive data.
- Regulatory Alignment: Stay updated on global regulations like GDPR to ensure compliance.

AI Model Management: Navigating the AI Lifecycle

Managing AI models is a dynamic process that spans their entire lifecycle—from development to retirement. Effective management ensures that AI systems are robust, ethical, and in line with organizational objectives.

Key Recommendations for AI Model Management

- **Model Tracking:** Legal Considerations in AI Model Tracking: Employ versioning systems to document changes, facilitating both rollback options and audit compliance.
- **Performance Monitoring:** Use automated metrics and KPIs to assess model effectiveness and fairness, enabling timely adjustments.

- **Strategic Updates:** Maintain a roadmap for model updates, outlining criteria for retirement or replacement to ensure ongoing relevance

The legal landscape for AI is intricate and varies significantly across jurisdictions. From data protection laws to intellectual property rights, businesses must navigate a labyrinth of regulations. Non-compliance not only risks legal repercussions but can also damage a company's reputation and stakeholder trust.

Unified Guidelines for Ethical and Compliant AI Governance

Recommendations for Streamlined AI Governance

1. **Data Governance:**
- **Quality Assurance:** Regularly audit and validate data for accuracy through periodic checks and data cleansing.
- **Privacy Protocols:** Utilise encryption and anonymisation techniques to protect sensitive data.
- **Regulatory Alignment:** Stay updated on global regulations like GDPR and align your data governance policies accordingly.
2. **AI Model Management:**
- **Model Tracking:** Employ versioning systems for documenting changes, facilitating both rollback and audit compliance.
- **Performance Monitoring:** Use automated metrics and KPIs for ongoing assessment of model effectiveness and fairness.
- **Strategic Updates:** Maintain a roadmap for model updates, outlining criteria for retirement or replacement.

3. **Legal Considerations:**

- **Stay Informed:** Keep a dynamic register of global AI compliance requirements and consult it for significant AI-related decisions.
- **Legal Partnerships:** Collaborate with legal experts specialising in AI and technology law for guidance on complex legal aspects.

4. **Ethical AI Practices:**

- **Bias Checks:** Continuously monitor for biases in both training data and AI-generated outcomes.
- **Ethical Guidelines:** Adhere to recognised ethical standards or frameworks specific to your industry or general principles like fairness and accountability.
- **Diverse Development:** Involve a range of perspectives, including ethicists and representatives from marginalised communities, in the AI development process.

Conclusion

In the rapidly evolving landscape of AI, effective governance is not just a regulatory requirement but a cornerstone for ethical and responsible AI deployment. By adhering to these unified guidelines, organisations can navigate the complexities of AI with increased assurance, ethical rigour, and compliance. The next chapter will focus on the AI Act and its implications for regulation, further enriching our understanding of AI governance.

Footnotes

1. " 5 Damaging Consequences Of A Data Breach by James MacKay " https://www.metacompliance.com/blog/data-breaches/5-damaging-consequences-of-a-data-breach#:~:text=A%20data%20breach%20can%20easily,accounts%20or%20making%20unauthorised%20purchases.

19. Chapter 19:

The AI Act and EU Proposed Regulation with a Comparative Look at U.S. Developments

Key Takeaways

1.**Pioneering Legislation:** The EU AI Act is set to become the world's first comprehensive law governing Artificial Intelligence, establishing a precedent for global AI regulation. It adopts a harm-based approach, classifying AI systems based on the potential risks they pose to society, a feature that sets it apart from other regulatory frameworks[1].

2.**Balancing Ethics and Innovation:** While the Act emphasizes strong ethical considerations, it also raises concerns among European businesses about potential limitations on innovation and global competitiveness. The Act aligns with international standards like ISO and CEN, contributing to global interoperability and best practices[2].

3.**Global Influence and U.S. Developments:** The Act is likely to shape AI regulations worldwide. Meanwhile, leading U.S. companies are voluntarily adopting risk management measures, signaling a move towards more robust AI regulation in the United States. The EU AI Act also influences international cooperation, as seen in Ireland's active participation in ISO and CEN committees[2].

Introduction

The landscape of Artificial Intelligence (AI) is undergoing a transformative shift, necessitating robust governance and regulatory frameworks. As AI technologies permeate diverse industries, the stakes for ethical considerations, business implications, and global policy ramifications escalate. This chapter offers an in-depth exploration of the EU's pioneering AI Act of 2023, a legislation that adopts a unique harm-based approach to AI regulation[1]. Alongside, we delve into the proactive measures taken by leading U.S. companies in the absence of comprehensive federal laws. Drawing on insights from my recent podcast interview with Aditya Mohan, Senior Scientific Officer from the National Standards Authority of Ireland, we will examine the Act's alignment with international standards like ISO and CEN, contributing to its global influence[2]. By the chapter's conclusion, readers will acquire a multifaceted understanding of the evolving landscape of AI regulation and its far-reaching consequences.

The AI Act

The European Union's AI Act serves as a groundbreaking legislative framework aimed at harmonizing the governance of Artificial Intelligence across its member states. The Act adopts a nuanced, harm-based approach to risk categorization, dividing AI systems into four distinct tiers: unacceptable, high, limited, and minimal risk. High-risk systems are subject to rigorous assessment protocols and must fulfill exhaustive documentation requirements prior to market entry. This aligns with the NSAI's (National Standards Authority of Ireland) contributions to international standards like ISO and CEN, ensuring that the Act is in line with global best practices[2]. Beyond mere risk assessment, the Act ambitiously aims to make AI technologies operationally transparent, decisions traceable, and impactfully non-discriminatory.

Ethical Considerations

The EU AI Act goes beyond regulatory compliance to embed ethical principles into the AI governance framework. It is committed to safeguarding public health, safety, and fundamental human rights. This ethical focus is informed by contributions from a national committee of AI experts, including those from the NSAI, who participate at the ISO level[2]. The Act also restricts member states from imposing unilateral limitations on AI systems, ensuring a harmonized approach unless explicit authorization is granted. The legislation has been fine-tuned through amendments to address ethical and practical challenges across sectors like healthcare, transport, and public services.

Businesses Reservations and Concerns of Regulation

19..1. Technological Sovereignty

European firms, particularly start-ups and SMEs, have expressed concerns that the Act's stringent regulations could hinder innovation and global competitiveness. These concerns are echoed by the NSAI, which emphasizes the importance of interoperability and alignment with international standards[2]. An open letter from over 160 executives has also highlighted these reservations, arguing that the Act could jeopardize Europe's technological sovereignty.

Global Regulatory Landscape in AI

The EU's top-down regulatory approach is contrasted by other countries adopting unique strategies. The NSAI's contributions to ISO and CEN standards indicate a preference for international alignment. Countries like Brazil and Japan are at different stages of regulatory development, each adopting unique approaches. The lack of global consensus on AI regulation underscores the need for a harmonized approach, as some industry leaders call for a pause on the development of Large Language Models to allow regulation to catch up.

U.S. Developments in AI Regulation

19..1. Voluntary Safeguards

In the absence of comprehensive federal legislation, seven leading U.S. companies, including Amazon, Google, and Microsoft, initially took the initiative to manage AI risks voluntarily. Their proactive measures have set a precedent, inspiring an additional eight firms, including Palantir, to follow suit. These companies have committed to a range of safeguards such as security testing, watermarking AI-generated content, and issuing regular public reports on the capabilities and limitations of their AI technologies.

19..1.1. Legislative Landscape

As of 2023, the U.S. has seen the introduction of several AI-related laws, primarily as components of broader consumer privacy legislation. These laws regulate AI and automated decision-making by offering users the option to opt-out of profiling and mandating impact assessments. This legislative approach reflects a growing awareness of the need to balance technological advancement with consumer rights and ethical considerations.

Executive Order

The U.S. administration is in the advanced stages of drafting an executive order to further regulate AI. Although the specifics are yet to be disclosed, the order is expected to focus on key areas like ethical considerations, data privacy, and national security. This forthcoming executive order could also provide federal agencies with guidelines on the implementation and oversight of AI technologies. This development underscores the U.S. government's acknowledgement of the increasing influence and associated risks of AI, as well as its intent to create a regulatory framework that may serve as a model for other jurisdictions.

International Collaboration

In a move that signifies the global implications of AI, the White House has announced its intention to collaborate with international allies to establish a global framework for AI governance. This initiative aims to create international standards that address ethical considerations, data governance, and responsible AI use. Such a collaborative approach could pave the way for a more harmonised regulatory landscape, thereby easing the compliance burden for companies operating across multiple countries.

The European Union's Regulatory Framework for AI

The AI Act: A Cornerstone of EU Digital Strategy

The European Union is proposing the AI Act as a pioneering step in AI regulation. This comprehensive legislation aims to govern the development and usage of AI across EU member states. It emphasises:

- **Safety:** Aligned with the European Parliament's vision, the Act prioritises human oversight to ensure a high level of protection for health, safety, and fundamental rights.
- **Efficiency:** The Act promotes the efficient use of AI technologies, aiming to make AI systems transparent, traceable, and non-discriminatory.
- **Sustainability:** Upholding environmental preservation is a key focus, encouraging sustainable practices in AI development.

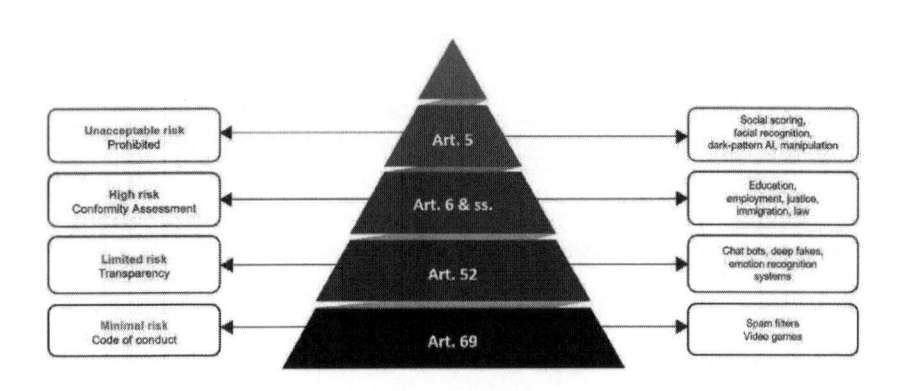

Figure 19.1 The Proposed EU AI Act

Risk-Based Regulatory Approach

The Act introduces a tiered, risk-based approach to AI regulation:

- **Unacceptable Risk:** AI systems posing this level of risk are banned.
- **High-Risk:** These AI systems are subject to rigorous assessment and proper documentation before market entry.
- **Minimal Risk:** Such AI systems must comply with minimal transparency requirements, enabling users to make informed decisions.

Recommendations

Below are recommendations aimed at helping businesses navigate the intricacies of the European Union's Artificial Intelligence Act. These guidelines cover compliance, strategic planning, ethical considerations, and future-proofing against the evolving backdrop of AI regulation.

Regulatory Compliance

1. **Risk Assessment:** Assess your AI systems to categorise them in line with the Act's risk tiers (unacceptable, high, limited, minimal). This will inform your compliance strategy.
2. **Documentation:** For high-risk AI systems, maintain thorough documentation that includes testing protocols, data quality, and human oversight mechanisms.

Strategic Planning

1. **Legal Consultation:** Consult legal experts who specialise in EU regulations to gauge your compliance obligations and potential liabilities under the Act.
2. **Budget Allocation:** Set aside financial resources for compliance measures, including technology audits and potential fines, which can be substantial.

Ethical Considerations

1. **Ethical Guidelines:** Develop or update ethical guidelines in alignment with the Act's focus on human rights and safety. This will aid in building trust with stakeholders.
2. **Stakeholder Engagement:** Involve key stakeholders, such as employees and customers, in ethical discussions about AI usage to ensure a more comprehensive approach.

Future-Proofing

1. **Monitoring Regulatory Changes:** Keep abreast of any amendments to the Act, as it is still under negotiation and subject to change.
2. **Global Implications:** Consider how compliance with the EU's regulations could influence your operations globally, as the Act is likely to set a precedent for other jurisdictions.

By proactively addressing these areas, businesses can not only ensure compliance but also position themselves as leaders in ethical and responsible AI usage.

Author's Insights: Navigating the Regulatory Landscape of AI

In a series of enlightening dialogues, I had the opportunity to engage with experts in the field of AI regulation. One discussion featured Dave Lewis, Associate Professor from the ADAPT Centre, and Brian McElligott, Head of AI at Mason Hayes & Curran[3]. We explored the intricacies of the EU's AI Act, which focuses on stringent criteria for high-risk AI systems and aligns closely with GDPR for consumer data protection. In a separate conversation, I spoke with Aditya Mohan, Senior Scientific Officer from the National Standards Authority Ireland[3]. Aditya provided valuable insights into the harmonization efforts within the EU and the role of national committees in contributing to ISO standards2. Collectively, these experts agree that both the EU and the U.S. are making significant strides in establishing a regulated environment for AI. However, their approaches reflect different priorities, influenced by their respective socio-political landscapes.

As AI continues to evolve, it's clear that these regulatory frameworks will also need to adapt to keep pace with technological advancements.

Conclusion

The proposed EU AI Act of 2023 and the recent commitments by leading U.S. companies are significant milestones in AI regulation. Drawing on insights from my podcast conversations with Dave Lewis of the ADAPT Centre and Brian McElligott of Mason Hayes & Curran[2], it's clear that while the EU aims to set high ethical and safety standards, there are valid concerns about its potential impact on innovation and global competitiveness. Meanwhile, the U.S. is also making strides towards more robust AI regulation. A balanced approach, involving all stakeholders, is crucial for the success of these regulatory frameworks. Our next chapter will delve into the often-overlooked hidden costs of AI projects, offering a comprehensive view of what businesses should consider before embarking on AI implementations.

Footnotes

1. " Navigating the EU AI Act: Implications for Financial Institutions " https://www.dechert.com/knowledge/onpoint/2023/7/navigating-the-eu-ai-act--implications-for-financial-institution.html#:~:text=These%20AI%20systems%20should%20comply,informed%20decisions%20about%20their%20interactions.

2. AI and the European Regulatory Landscape: A Podcast Discussion with Dave Lewis and Brian McElligott" (Podcast URL https://aiireland.ie/2023/05/09/e103-the-ai-act/#more-19518)

3. The AI Ireland Podcast with Aditya Mohan NSAI - Ireland's Role in Shaping International AI Standards", based on podcast interview with Aditya Mohan, Senior Scientific Officer from National Standards Authority Ireland. https://aiireland.ie/2023/09/21/e112-aditya-mohan-senior-scientific-officer-at-the-national-standards-authority-of-ireland/

20. Chapter 20:

Unmasking the Hidden Costs of AI – Liability, Risks, and Financial Considerations

Key Takeaways

1. Holistic Cost Assessment: Beyond the obvious financial investments, the hidden costs of AI integration can be substantial. These include legal liabilities, ongoing training, and data protection measures. Understanding these costs is crucial for successful AI implementation.

2. Ethical and Legal Preparedness: Ethical considerations and legal complexities are not just optional but essential components of responsible AI use. Organisations must stay updated on emerging regulations and ethical best practices to mitigate risks effectively.

3. Continuous Adaptation and Learning: AI is a rapidly evolving field. Organisations must invest in continuous learning programs and risk assessment tools to adapt to technological advancements and ethical considerations. This ongoing commitment is key to long-term success and responsible AI integration.

Introduction

Throughout this book, I've highlighted the transformative potential and high ROI of AI. However, the journey to these rewards is complex and fraught with challenges. Initial costs for hardware, software, and talent can be significant, but the long-term benefits often justify these investments. This chapter serves as a guide to the less obvious but equally critical aspects of AI projects: the risks, liabilities, and hidden financial considerations. Given the unique nature of each AI initiative, my aim is to provide you with the knowledge to navigate these complexities effectively. From legal pitfalls to ethical dilemmas, this chapter will offer a comprehensive yet concise overview to help you make informed decisions in your AI endeavours.

Section 1: Financial Aspects of AI Integration

20..1. The Financial Commitment of Integrating AI into Business Operations

When contemplating the adoption of AI into your business model, the initial financial outlay is often the first hurdle. This isn't merely a software investment; it encompasses hardware, software licenses, and crucially, the recruitment of skilled professionals. While machine learning is permeating various industries, gauging the actual costs can be complex. To run AI algorithms effectively, specialized hardware is essential, capable of managing the large data volumes and complex calculations. According to an article by Centerbase, a mid-range server could set you back more than $10,000, with an additional $2,000 or so needed for a backup system[1].

Financial Commitment: A Comparative Lens

Understanding the financial obligations associated with AI integration is a pivotal element for businesses. While the initial financial outlay can be considerable, it's vital to assess these expenditures within a broader framework. Insights gathered from in-depth interviews with industry leaders reveal that the ROI and initial capital deployed in AI often surpass those of other technological options. Although the upfront financial commitment for AI may appear daunting, the long-term economic benefits, such as automation, operational efficiency, and data-driven decision-making, frequently validate the investment. This comparative analysis equips business leaders to make well-informed choices, juxtaposing the costs and advantages of AI against other technological solutions. Hence, comprehending the financial landscape through a comparative lens is not merely recommended but essential for sustained success in AI adoption.

Nonetheless, a 2021 PWC survey indicates that numerous organizations struggle to achieve a meaningful financial return on their AI investments, with some not even reaching the break-even point[2]. According to the McKinsey Global Survey on the state of AI in 2021, companies that have effectively implemented and integrated AI have seen substantial ROI improvements across multiple facets of their business operations[3].

20..2. Case Study: IBM's AI Adoption

Consider IBM's case as an illustration. The company's transition to AI-based operations was far from trivial; the hardware expenses alone are said to be around an astounding $2 million. In the industry these upfront costs are regarded as 'day-zero expenses,' emphasising the financial readiness required for businesses before diving into AI.

20..3. Operational Expenses: The Costs You Didn't See Coming

Once you've made the initial investment, you might think the heavy lifting is over. However, the operational expenses that follow can be just as demanding. These are the costs that often don't make it into the initial budget but are crucial for the long-term success of the project. We're talking about system maintenance, model training, and even data-related costs like acquisition and compliance. To put it in perspective, Amazon is rumoured to spend roughly $1.2 million annually just to maintain data quality. Experts warns of the engineering challenges that come with transitioning an AI project from a proof of concept to a production-ready application.

ROI Realities: Balancing Costs and Benefits

The ultimate question for any business leader is, "Will this investment pay off?" Calculating the return on investment (ROI) for AI projects is not straightforward. While the benefits can be transformative, the costs—both upfront and ongoing—can be substantial. Businesses need to be cognizant of both visible and hidden costs, including ethical and legal considerations, when calculating ROI. Another layer to this discussion is the importance of a data-centric approach. focusing on high-quality data can yield better results than merely building complex models.

Navigating the financial landscape of AI integration is a complex but essential task for any forward-thinking business leader. Being aware of both the upfront and hidden costs, as well as having a realistic expectation of ROI, can make the difference between a successful AI project and a costly misstep.

Section 2: Operational Adjustments

20..1. Operational Adjustments: The Need for Organisational Changes

Integrating AI into your business isn't just a matter of installing new software; it often necessitates a shift in organisational structure and workflow. Companies may need to upskill their current staff or even hire new talent specifically trained in AI and data analytics. Harvard Business Review emphasises the importance of a data-centric approach, suggesting that companies should shift their engineering focus from model-centric to data-centric approaches[4].

Section 3: Hidden Costs

20..1. Hidden Costs: The Expenses You Didn't Anticipate

While the upfront and operational costs of AI are often discussed, hidden costs like continuous learning and updates can catch businesses off guard. Google's DeepMind, for example, requires ongoing investment in research and development. Similarly, Amazon faces hidden costs in maintaining data quality, which can run into the millions annually.

Section 4: Legal Complexities

20..1. Liability Challenges: Navigating the Legal Maze

Determining liability in the world of AI is a complex issue. Take Tesla's self-driving cars as an example. Incidents involving these vehicles raise questions about whether the fault lies with the human driver, the AI system, or the company itself.

Ethical and Legal Preparedness: The Human Element

In the rapidly evolving landscape of AI ethics and regulations, organisations are increasingly

recognising the need for dedicated ethics committees. These committees act as internal think tanks, interpreting and implementing new guidelines and best practices. Drawing from extensive interviews with industry leaders, it's evident that such committees serve as a crucial safeguard against potential legal pitfalls and ethical dilemmas. By proactively addressing these issues, organizations can not only mitigate risks but also set a standard for responsible AI use.

20..2. Future Legal Landscape: Staying Ahead of the Curve

As AI technologies evolve, so do the legal frameworks governing them. Companies must stay updated on emerging regulations to mitigate risks and ensure compliance.

Section 5: Risk Management

20..1. AI Insurance: Safeguarding Your Investment

As AI becomes more integrated into business operations, the need for specialised insurance policies grows. Companies are starting to pioneer in this space, offering AI-specific insurance policies to mitigate potential risks.

20..2. Risk Assessment Tools: Quantifying the Unknown

Tools like RiskLens are emerging to help businesses quantify the financial impact of potential risks associated with AI integration. These tools can be invaluable in preparing for and mitigating risks.

Section 6: Ethical Concerns: The Reputational Aspect

20..1. Ethical Concerns: Balancing Innovation and Responsibility

Addressing ethical concerns in AI is not merely a matter of compliance; it's a matter of corporate reputation. Drawing from my involvement in the AI Awards, which showcase responsible AI applications, it's evident that companies that proactively tackle ethical issues not only mitigate risks but also enhance their brand value. This focus on ethical responsibility serves as a differentiator in the market, attracting both consumer trust and investor interest. Therefore, the reputational aspect of ethical AI practices should not be overlooked but rather integrated into a company's overall AI strategy. It's also important to address biases and ensure fairness in AI outputs, which requires substantial resources. Navigating the complexities of AI integration requires a multi-faceted approach, covering everything from financial and operational considerations to legal and ethical responsibilities. Being well-informed and prepared can make the difference between a successful AI strategy and a costly misadventure.

20..2. Sustainable AI: The Green Side of Intelligence

The environmental footprint of AI is an often-overlooked aspect that deserves attention. Data centres powering AI algorithms consume significant amounts of energy, contributing to the global carbon footprint. Companies like Google are leading the way in sustainability initiatives, aiming to operate entirely on carbon-free energy by 2030[5]. These efforts not only mitigate the environmental impact but also set a precedent for other companies to follow.

Author's Insights

In one of my inaugural interviews for the AI Ireland Podcast back in 2018, I had the opportunity to speak with Adam Bermingham, the then Engineering Lead at Zalando. Adam shared invaluable insights into how Zalando successfully bridged the gap between data science and data engineering to generate a significant return on investment (ROI). The episode serves as an excellent resource, shedding light on engineering principles that not only generate ROI but also reduce costs[6].

This conversation underscores the imperative of continuous learning in the ever-evolving landscape of AI. It's not merely a technological requirement but also an ethical one. As AI systems become increasingly integrated into societal frameworks, the need for ongoing updates and ethical considerations becomes paramount. Businesses must commit to not just updating their algorithms but also regularly revisiting the ethical implications of their AI applications.

Recommendations

1. Financial Planning: Ensure a comprehensive understanding of both upfront and hidden costs before embarking on an AI project.

2. Legal Preparedness: Stay updated on emerging legal frameworks and consider liability insurance specific to AI.

3. Ethical Responsibility: Implement ethical guidelines and conduct regular audits to ensure AI applications are bias-free and fair.

4. Environmental Consciousness: Consider the environmental impact of your AI operations and explore sustainable options.

Conclusion

Navigating the labyrinthine landscape of AI integration is far more than a financial endeavour; it's a multi-dimensional challenge requiring a comprehensive strategy. This strategy must encompass not just capital investment but also operational realignment, legal due diligence, robust risk management, ethical governance, and a commitment to environmental sustainability.

Being well-versed in these dimensions is not optional; it's a necessity. It's the linchpin that distinguishes a transformative AI strategy from a costly misadventure. Therefore, businesses must adopt a holistic approach that transcends mere technological implementation. This involves a commitment to continuous learning and agile adaptation in both technological and ethical spheres, all informed by real-world data and stakeholder input.

As we transition to our next chapter focusing on the application of AI in cybersecurity, it becomes imperative for business leaders to pay meticulous attention. The cybersecurity landscape represents a critical frontier in AI applications, and understanding its intricacies could be the key to safeguarding not just your data but also your brand's integrity.

To assist you in this complex journey, we've included a comprehensive AI Integration Checklist in Appendix A1. This checklist serves as a practical guide, covering the multi-dimensional challenges of AI, from financial investment to ethical considerations. We strongly recommend consulting it as you formulate or refine your AI strategy.

Footnotes

1. Cost Breakdown of Cloud and On-Premises Software

https://centerbase.com/blog/cost-breakdown-of-cloud-and-on-premise-software/

2 PWC AI Business Survey 2021 https://www.pwc.com/us/en/tech-effect/ai-analytics/ai-business-survey.html

3. McKinsey Survey on the State of AI in 2021
https://www.mckinsey.com/~/media/McKinsey/Business%20Functions/McKinsey%20Analytics/Our%20Insights/Global%20survey%20The%20state%20of%20AI%20in%202021/Global-survey-The-state-of-AI-in-2021.pdf

4. Reskilling in the Age of AI by Jorge Tamayo – HBR - https://hbr.org/2023/09/reskilling-in-the-age-of-ai

5. Google Research by David Patterson Good News about the carbon footprint of machine learning training February 2022 https://blog.research.google/2022/02/good-news-about-carbon-footprint-of.html

6. Adam Bermingham Zalando Interview AI Ireland https://aiawards.ie/e05-adam-bermingham-zalando/

7. 'AI Integration Checklist' [Source: Appendix A]

21. Chapter 21:

Ethical and Economic Implications of AI in Cybersecurity

Key Takeaways

1.**Immediate ROI in Cybersecurity:** The global cybersecurity market was valued at USD 202.72 billion in 2022 and is expected to grow at a CAGR of 12.3% from 2023 to 2030[1]. This underscores the immediate return on investment (ROI) that AI can bring specifically to cybersecurity initiatives.

2.**Strategic Leadership in Cybersecurity:** Companies guided by executives who have a deep understanding of AI's role in cybersecurity are better positioned to mitigate risks and maximize profits. This leadership is crucial in navigating the complex landscape of cyber threats and AI-driven solutions.

3.**AI vs. AI in Cybersecurity:** The cybersecurity landscape is evolving into a battleground where businesses face threats not just from human hackers but also from AI-powered cyber-attacks. Understanding this dynamic is essential for effective defense strategies.

Introduction

In the age of digital transformation, AI is not just a technological tool; it represents a paradigm shift that requires a change in organisational mindset and culture. This is particularly true in the realm of cybersecurity, where AI can either be a formidable ally or a potential vulnerability. This chapter aims to equip business executives with actionable insights for successfully integrating AI into their cybersecurity strategies, thereby enhancing both risk mitigation and profit maximisation.

The Economic Imperative of AI in Cybersecurity

The market value of AI in cybersecurity goes beyond mere statistics; it serves as a compelling testament to the immediate return on investment (ROI) that businesses can realise. Far from being a nascent field, cybersecurity powered by AI is a rapidly evolving industry. When leveraged effectively, it can transform from a cost center to a significant profit center for your organisation. This evolution is driven by AI's ability to automate complex tasks, thereby reducing operational costs, while simultaneously enhancing the effectiveness of cybersecurity measures.

Case Studies: Real-World Applications and Lessons Learned

Drawing from my extensive interviews with industry leaders, it's clear that the theoretical aspects of AI in cybersecurity are only part of the story. For instance, my conversation with Des Ryan, Former Director of Cyber Security at Microsoft Ireland, revealed how the company uses AI to detect and respond to threats in real-time, thereby significantly reducing the potential damage from cyber-attacks[2]. Similarly, Jimmy Hennessy, SVP of Data Science at ACI Worldwide, shared how AI algorithms are used to predict fraudulent activities, offering a proactive approach to cybersecurity[2]. In a recent podcast interview, Pawel Lee, Principal Data Scientist at North American Bancard, delved into the day-to-day work of his team, focusing on consumer fraud monitoring[3]. Lee emphasized the importance of defining the right problems to solve and discussed ongoing projects aimed at combating financial fraud on the Dark Web. These insights offer a unique perspective on the practical challenges and opportunities in using AI for cybersecurity, particularly in the financial sector.

Future Trends: The Evolving Landscape of AI and Cybersecurity

The cybersecurity landscape is continuously evolving, with AI and machine learning at the forefront of innovation and threat mitigation. However, emerging technologies like quantum computing and blockchain are set to further reshape this domain.

AI-Driven Security

Advanced AI algorithms will increasingly enable proactive security measures, allowing organisations to anticipate and mitigate threats before they become critical issues.

Quantum Computing

This technology presents both opportunities for stronger encryption and risks of breaking existing security protocols. Businesses must prepare for these quantum capabilities to maintain security integrity.

Blockchain in Cybersecurity

The rise of blockchain offers new, secure ways to store and access data, opening doors for innovative AI applications in cybersecurity.

Understanding these trends is essential for any organisation aiming to maintain a robust cybersecurity posture whilst leveraging AI's transformative potential.

Author's Insights: Navigating the Future of AI in Cybersecurity

In my engagements with industry leaders, the view of AI stands as a double-edged sword, part solution and part challenge. Nevertheless, the prevailing sentiment within the industry is one of optimism, particularly regarding AI's capacity to bolster security measures and deliver a strong return on investment (ROI). These insights were further enriched by a recent podcast interview with Pawel Lee, Principal Data Scientist at North American Bancard. Lee's emphasis on the quality of data and organisational culture mirrors the wider industry outlook, underscoring the necessity for a strategic and holistic approach to AI in cybersecurity.

As detailed in this chapter, it is clear that the future of cybersecurity is intrinsically linked with advancements in AI, as well as emergent technologies like quantum computing and blockchain. For organisations aiming to stay ahead, understanding and incorporating these trends into their cybersecurity strategy is not merely advisable; it is essential.

As we look to the future, those who will emerge as winners in this fast-evolving landscape will be the organisations that successfully align their business strategies with these technological advances. Such an alignment is not only pivotal for ensuring robust security but also for achieving a competitive advantage.

Recommendations

1. Strategic Talent Acquisition and Retention: Given the acute shortage of qualified AI professionals, it's imperative to adopt innovative recruitment and retention strategies. Consider partnerships with educational institutions for talent pipelines and offer continuous learning opportunities to keep your team updated and engaged.

2. Holistic Change Management: The successful integration of AI into cybersecurity goes beyond mere technological adoption; it requires a cultural shift and operational realignment. Executive leadership must spearhead this transformation, ensuring that it is aligned with broader business objectives and involves cross-functional teams for seamless execution.

3. Corporate Social Responsibility in AI: The Ireland AI Awards, which I founded, serve not just as a recognition platform but also as a catalyst for ethical AI practices. Participating in or sponsoring such initiatives not only enhances your corporate reputation but also contributes to the broader ecosystem of responsible AI applications.

Conclusion

The fusion of Artificial Intelligence with cybersecurity represents a seismic shift, fundamentally redefining how we safeguard digital assets. For today's business leaders, the challenge is not merely to adapt but to lead. The organisations that will thrive are those that strategically align AI initiatives with their broader business objectives and place a premium on robust data governance. As we segue into Part V and Chapter 22, we will delve into compelling real-world case studies that underscore the transformative power of AI across various industries. This chapter serves as more than a summation; it is a clarion call for proactive leadership. In the ever-fluid landscape of AI in cybersecurity, the onus is on decision-makers to steer their organisations with foresight and agility.

Footnotes

1. The global cyber security market size was estimated at USD 202.72 billion in 2022 and is projected to grow at a compound annual growth rate (CAGR) of 12.3% from 2023 to 2030 https://www.grandviewresearch.com/industry-analysis/cyber-security-market#:~:text=Report%20Overview,12.3%25%20from%202023%20to%202030

2. AI Irelad Podcast E78 Jimmy Hennessy Des Traynor Interview https://aiireland.ie/2021/12/16/e78-jimmy-hennessey-aci-worldwide/

3. " E107 Pawel Lee, Principal Data Scientist at North American Bancard E107 Pawel Lee, Principal Data Scientist at North American Bancard "

E107 Pawel Lee, Principal Data Scientist at North American Bancard

22. Chapter 22:

Case Studies of Successful AI Implementation

Key Takeaways

1. AI holds transformative power in areas like Healthcare, Finance, and Human Resources.

2. Targeting repetitive tasks and rich data fields maximises AI effectiveness.

3. Keeping up-to-date with AI innovations is crucial for making informed decisions and staying competitive.

Introduction

AI is quickly evolving and creating significant changes in fields like Healthcare, Finance, and Human Resources. Building on Part I, this chapter will showcase practical case studies demonstrating AI's impact. The focus is both global and local, with specific examples from Ireland. Through my role as CEO of AI Ireland, I've witnessed more than 500 AI applications that address real-world business and societal issues. In this chapter, we'll delve into some of these remarkable uses across various sectors.

Figure 22.1 Real World Applications of AI

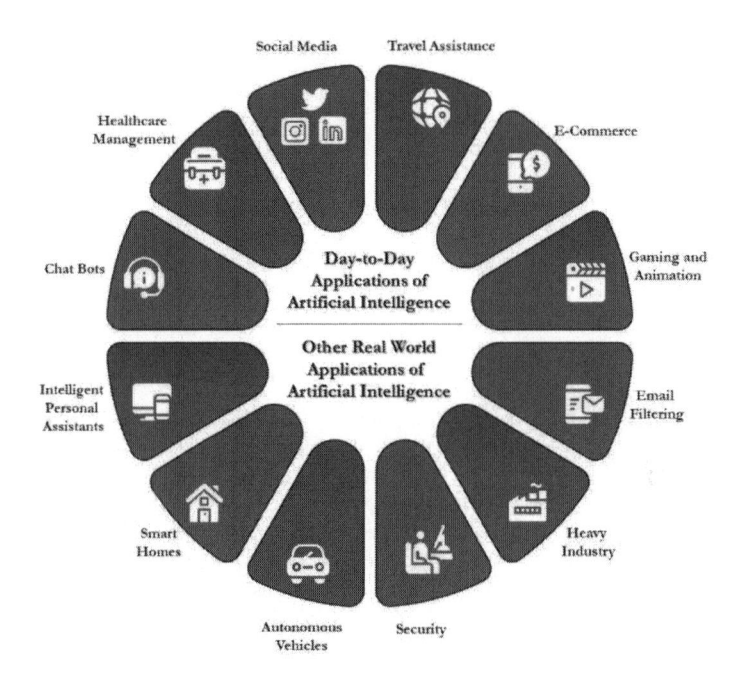

AI Case Studies

Section 1: Healthcare - Transforming Patient Care

1.1 Diagnostics

Irish Case Study: INFANT Research Centre

INFANT Research Centre in Ireland is a distinguished entity in healthcare AI. The centre employs AI to pinpoint seizures in newborns, giving clinicians efficient tools to better infant care. Not only does this technology enhance diagnostic reliability, but it also shows promise in reducing long-term health risks for infants[1].

INFANT has been honoured as a winner at the AI Awards on four separate occasions.

1.2 Administrative Efficiency

Insights from Healthcare Leaders

In dialogues with healthcare executives, it's clear that AI extends beyond patient care into administrative functions. AI-powered speech recognition is reducing administrative load by automating medical transcription. The technology is thereby contributing to streamlined operations and more efficient healthcare management.

Section 2: Finance - Streamlining Financial Operations

2.1 Fraud Detection

Irish Case Study: ACI Worldwide

ACI Worldwide is revolutionising fraud prevention in finance through its Incremental Learning technology. More details can be found in my podcast with Jimmy Hennessy where he shares his teams' applications for the winning prize at the AI Awards[2].

2.2 Investment Management

International Case Study: Wealthfront

Wealthfront uses AI-driven Robo-advisors to manage portfolios, democratising financial advice. Ethical considerations, such as responsible usage, should not be overlooked.

Section 3: Human Resources - Talent Management with AI

3.1 Employee Recognition and Performance

Irish Case Study: Workhuman

Workhuman uses machine learning to enhance employee recognition and performance.

3.2 Recruitment

International Case Study: HireVue

HireVue employs AI to streamline recruitment, reducing the time-to-hire and improving candidate quality.

Section 4: Marketing - Personalised Customer Experiences

4.1 Customer Engagement

Irish Case Study: Webio

Webio uses AI to deliver personalised experiences, from marketing messages to customer service interactions[3]. An AI Awards winner in 2022, they were recognised for their customer-centric approach and also their emphasis on an ethical approach to AI.

4.2 Campaign Optimisation

International Case Studies: Adobe Sensei and Salesforce Einstein

Both platforms utilise AI for real-time analytics, driving smarter marketing decisions.

Author's Insight

As the CEO of AI Ireland, I have the pleasure of meeting and speaking with the founders of over 500 AI Awards applications. Our discussions often revolve around how they have used a "problem worth solving" approach to add real value to users. This experience has provided me with a unique vantage point to observe the transformative impact of AI across multiple sectors.

Through these extensive interactions, I've seen firsthand how AI is not just a technological advancement but a tool that can solve complex societal issues when applied responsibly. Whether it's INFANT Research Centre's work in neonatal care[1] or ACI Worldwide's[2] efforts in fraud prevention, the case studies in this chapter exemplify the potential of AI to bring about meaningful change.

It's also worth noting that the ethical considerations surrounding AI are not mere afterthoughts; they are integral to the technology's responsible deployment. This is a recurring theme in my conversations with industry leaders and is reflected in the AI Awards' emphasis on ethical AI applications. The insights shared in this chapter are not just theoretical musings but are grounded in real-world applications and ethical considerations. They serve as a testament to the transformative power of AI when applied thoughtfully and responsibly.

Recommendations for Businesses

Ethical AI Use

Prioritise the ethical implementation of AI in all business operations. Develop a set of guidelines that address data privacy, fairness, and transparency to ensure responsible AI usage. Ethical considerations should be integral to your AI strategy to maintain consumer trust and mitigate legal risks.

Employee Upskilling

Invest in ongoing training programmes to help employees acquire the necessary skills to work alongside AI technologies. Such programmes not only boost productivity but also ensure that your workforce remains relevant in a rapidly evolving technological landscape.

Collaboration with Academia

Forge partnerships with academic institutions to gain access to cutting-edge research and top-tier talent. These collaborations can drive innovation, provide fresh perspectives, and facilitate the commercialisation of new AI technologies.

Customer-first Approach

Utilise AI to enhance customer experience by personalising interactions, improving product recommendations, and streamlining customer service. Make customer satisfaction a key performance indicator in assessing the success of AI implementations.

For Policymakers

1. **Regulatory Frameworks**

Develop comprehensive regulations that promote the ethical use of AI while also facilitating innovation. Standardised guidelines can provide a robust framework for businesses to operate within, reducing ambiguity and fostering responsible AI development.

2. **Innovation Incentives**

Offer tax incentives, grants, or subsidies to companies and educational institutions that contribute to AI innovation. Such incentives could stimulate research and development, leading to advancements that benefit society at large.

3. **National AI Strategy**

Formulate a cohesive national strategy for AI that aligns with the country's broader economic and social goals. This can serve as a roadmap for both the public and private sectors, helping to coordinate efforts and maximise the positive impact of AI technologies.

4. **Public-Private Partnership**

Encourage collaborations between governmental agencies and the private sector to address societal challenges through AI. These partnerships can expedite the deployment of AI solutions in areas such as healthcare, education, and infrastructure.

These recommendations aim to provide actionable steps for businesses and policymakers alike, focusing on responsible AI implementation, workforce development, and synergistic collaborations for societal benefit.

Conclusion

This chapter provided a comprehensive analysis of AI's role in multiple sectors, examining both its game-changing benefits and the ethical considerations that come into play. As AI continues to evolve at a rapid pace, it is crucial for decision-makers to stay current to make informed strategic choices. As we move on to Part VI, we will turn our focus toward the future of AI. We'll start by exploring how AI is redefining the future of work, then move on to discuss global AI strategies and competitiveness. This will be followed by insights into emerging trends and technologies in AI that are set to transform the business landscape. We'll also look at leadership strategies for an AI-centric future and conclude by outlining a roadmap for thriving in an era increasingly dictated by AI.

Our next chapter will specifically delve into the transformative impact AI is having on the world of work, serving as a foundation for the enriching discussions that will follow in Part VI.

Footnotes

1. " UCC-designed Brain Injury Detection Device secures Enterprise Ireland funding " https://www.ucc.ie/en/news/2022/ucc-designed-brain-injury-detection-device-secures-enterprise-ireland-funding.html

2. E78 AI Ireland Podcast ACI Jimmy Hennessy https://aiireland.ie/2021/12/16/e78-jimmy-hennessey-aci-worldwide/

3. " E20 AI Ireland Webio Podcast with Paul Sweeney https://aiawards.ie/e20-paul-sweeney-webio/

4. " Salesforce Einstein vs Microsoft Copilot vs HubSpot ChatSpot vs Adobe Sensei - Smart CRM AI Comparison 2023" https://www.streamcreative.com/blog/salesforce-einstein-vs-microsoft-copilot-vs-hubspot-chatspot-vs-adobe-sensei

23. Chapter 23:

The Future of Work with AI

Key Takeaways

1. AI will fundamentally reshape the workforce, creating both challenges and opportunities for businesses. Adaptation and reskilling are key.

2. Ethical considerations in AI will play a significant role in the future of work, affecting everything from hiring practices to employee engagement.

3. The global reach of AI means that its impact on the future of work will be felt worldwide, requiring international collaboration and new forms of cross-border partnerships.

Introduction: The AI Revolution Begins

In 2021, OpenAI's GPT-3 demonstrated the ability to write code, answer queries, and even compose poetry, highlighting the rapid pace and diverse capabilities of AI. The technology is advancing at an unprecedented rate, making it crucial for executives to stay ahead of the curve. Understanding AI's capabilities can be a significant asset in strategic planning. This chapter aims to explore the transformative impact of AI on the future of work, from its role as a collaborative partner in the workplace to the ethical considerations that accompany its implementation.

We shall delve into these aspects and more, providing a comprehensive understanding of how AI is reshaping the future of work.

AI as a Collaborative Partner in the Workplace

The advent of generative AI, exemplified by OpenAI's ChatGPT, has made AI more relevant to workers than ever before. This technology serves as a collaborative partner, assisting in tasks ranging from writing cover letters to generating art. AI is not merely a tool; it acts as a force multiplier for human intelligence and productivity, enhancing various sectors including coding, marketing, legal, and healthcare administration. For business executives, understanding this collaborative nature of AI can offer a strategic advantage, leading to more efficient decision-making and increased employee productivity.

Navigating the AI Landscape: A Comprehensive Dive into the Future of Work

AI's role extends beyond that of a mere tool; it is a strategic collaborator that can offer insights based on data analytics. This partnership can lead to more informed business decisions and a more agile company

The Role Reversal

The future will see humans assisting AI, not the other way around. This requires a new mindset focused on collaboration rather than competition. Businesses should prepare for this shift by training employees in AI literacy and fostering a culture of collaboration between human workers and AI systems.

Expanding Ideas and Solutions

Generative AI can function as a personal assistant, aiding knowledge workers in expanding and analysing their work. Carl Benedikt Frey, the Future of Work Director at Oxford University, points out that AI can help brainstorm new ideas, test counterarguments to a thesis, and even write an abstract for research[1]. This means that for executives and knowledge workers, AI can assist in creating business plans, distilling complex topics for target audiences, and even predicting project costs and timelines.

AI's Revolutionary Impact

AI's transformative power is poised to redefine business operations from the ground up. It's not just about automating tasks but transforming entire business models. Companies that adapt quickly to this revolution will be the ones that thrive in the new landscape.

AI's Expansive Reach

As elaborated in Chapter 22, AI's influence is ubiquitous, spanning from healthcare, where it powers diagnostic algorithms, to finance, where robot-advisors are becoming increasingly prevalent. This widespread application is levelling the playing field, making services more universally accessible. Such democratisation has the potential to unlock new business opportunities and revenue channels.

AI as a Sounding Board

Generative AI also serves as a sounding board for idea generation. Ethan Mollick, an associate professor at the University of Pennsylvania, uses

AI to help process information and summarize content[2]. For business executives, this means AI can be a valuable partner in strategic planning and decision-making, offering a different perspective and helping to process large volumes of information more efficiently.

Efficiency in White-Collar Jobs

AI impacts not just what we do but who we are, affecting our work-related identities and roles within organizations. This shift can lead to more engaged employees who feel their skills are being augmented by AI, rather than replaced. It's crucial for companies to manage this transition carefully to maintain employee satisfaction and productivity.

The GenAI Adaptation

AI-driven learning platforms are making lifelong learning more accessible, tailored, and efficient. These platforms can be integrated into corporate training programs, offering personalised learning paths for employees. This can lead to a more skilled and adaptable workforce, ready to meet the challenges of the AI era.

Ethical Implications of AI in the Workplace

Ethical considerations like algorithmic bias and data privacy are crucial for building trust and compliance. Companies should establish AI ethics committees and invest in transparency tools. This proactive approach to ethics can serve as a differentiator in the market, attracting both customers and top talent.

Increasing Accuracy and Addressing Biases

AI has the capability to identify issues that humans might overlook, such as inaccuracies in text or biases in data interpretation. Anna Salomons, a professor at Utrecht University School of Economics, explains that while AI can identify problems, humans are still needed to correct them[3]. For executives, this means that AI can serve as a tool for impartial analysis, helping to make more informed and unbiased decisions.

Training, Reskilling, and the Global Perspective

AI's impact is global, necessitating international collaboration for training and reskilling workers. Companies should look beyond their local markets to understand the global implications of AI. Cross-border partnerships can offer new opportunities for growth and innovation.

McKinsey's Insights: The Changing American Work Landscape

By 2030, up to 30% of work hours could be automated, but AI is more likely to augment roles in STEM, creative fields, and business rather than replace them outright[4]. This augmentation will create new job roles that we haven't even imagined yet. Companies should start preparing for this future by identifying the skills that will be most valuable in an AI-augmented workforce.

The Future Job Landscape

While there are concerns about AI replacing jobs, experts suggest that AI could actually create new job opportunities. Data from the World Economic Forum indicates that AI and machine learning specialists are among the fastest-growing job fields[5]. For business executives, this implies that while AI will disrupt traditional job roles, it will also create new roles that we can't yet imagine, requiring a proactive approach to workforce planning and development.

Author's Insights

As the Co-Founder of an AI Staffing firm, my perspective on the future of work is deeply influenced by the real-world applications of AI in talent acquisition and management. The transformative power of AI is not just theoretical; it's a reality that businesses are experiencing today. AI is not merely a tool for automation but a strategic partner that can significantly enhance human capabilities. It's reshaping how we think about talent, from sourcing and recruiting to ongoing employee engagement and development. Companies that embrace this AI-driven paradigm shift will not only survive but thrive in the rapidly evolving landscape of the future of work.

Challenges, Limitations, and the Road Ahead

While AI offers numerous benefits, challenges like data security and job displacement exist. Solutions like AI audits can help navigate these issues. It's essential for companies to have a risk mitigation strategy in place to address these challenges proactively.

Recommendations

Invest in Employee Reskilling and AI Literacy: Given the transformative role of AI in the workplace, it's crucial for businesses to invest in employee training programs focused on AI literacy and adaptability. This will not only prepare your workforce for the AI-augmented future but also foster a culture of continuous learning and innovation.

Establish an AI Ethics Committee: As AI becomes more integrated into business operations, ethical considerations like algorithmic bias and data privacy can't be overlooked. Establishing an AI ethics committee can help your organization navigate these complex issues, build trust with both employees and customers, and differentiate your brand in the market.

Adopt a Global Perspective on AI's Impact: The influence of AI is not confined to local or national boundaries; it's a global phenomenon. Companies should seek international collaborations and cross-border partnerships to better understand the global implications of AI. This will enable you to tap into new markets and innovation ecosystems, enriching your business strategy.

Conclusion: Charting the AI Era

The promise of AI in shaping the future of work is immense, yet it comes with the imperative for businesses to act both proactively and ethically. Companies at the forefront of AI adoption are not merely adopting new technologies; they are setting the benchmarks for industry standards and ethical best practices. For executives, the mandate is clear: staying ahead of the AI curve is not an option but a necessity for ensuring operational efficiency and ethical integrity. In the upcoming chapter, we will delve deeper into how businesses can navigate the global AI landscape, achieve market dominance, foster sustainable development, and secure long-term strategic competitiveness.

Footnotes

1. " The future of Employment: How susceptible are jobs to computerisation? "
https://www.oxfordmartin.ox.ac.uk/downloads/academic/The_Future_of_Employment.pdf

2. Forward Thinking on the brave new world of Generative AI with Ethan Mollick
https://www.mckinsey.com/mgi/forward-thinking/forward-thinking-on-the-brave-new-world-of-generative-ai-with-ethan-mollick

3. Workplace AI:How Artificial Intelligence will transform the workday. Prof. Dr. Anna Salomons- Utrecht University
https://www.bbc.com/worklife/article/20230515-workplace-ai-how-artificial-intelligence-will-transform-the-workday#:~:text=The%20ability%20to%20%E2%80%9Cmore%20quickly,more%20accurately%20than%20humans%20alone.

4. " Generative AI and the future of work in America "
https://www.mckinsey.com/mgi/our-research/generative-ai-and-the-future-of-work-in-america

5. The Future of Jobs Reports 2023 The World Economic Forum
https://www.weforum.org/reports/the-future-of-jobs-report-2023/digest/

24. Chapter 24:

Navigating the Global AI Landscape for Executives

Key Takeaways

1. AI's global influence is reshaping economic, military, and strategic sectors.

2. The success of AI's global implementation hinges on understanding local regulations, market dynamics, cultural norms, and technological infrastructure.

3. Adapting to these local contexts is essential for a successful and ethical AI deployment.

Introduction

The global ascent of Artificial Intelligence (AI) is reshaping the way nations and businesses operate and strategise. As countries intensify their AI initiatives, executives must grasp the multifaceted factors that mould the global AI landscape. Moreover, gaining actionable insights and simple solutions are crucial for effective navigation. To this end, developing a Global AI Strategy can serve as a foundational step for executives, providing a flexible yet robust framework to guide the organisation's AI initiatives across different geographies.

The Major Players in AI

The global AI stage features prominent players, each bringing unique strengths:

- **USA:** The US, home to innovation hubs like Silicon Valley, has been a leader in AI. Its vast resources in capital and talent have spurred the growth of numerous AI start-ups and tech giants. Given the US's influence, executives should consider establishing a dedicated compliance team to keep abreast of American data protection and AI ethics laws, as these often-set global standards[1].
- **China:** China is rapidly advancing in AI, driven by tech giants like Alibaba and Tencent. Significant government investment in AI R&D further fuels this growth. For businesses looking to expand into China, understanding the local regulatory environment is crucial. Executives should consider forming strategic partnerships with local entities to gain invaluable insights into market dynamics and regulations[2].
- **Europe:** Europe boasts a thriving AI ecosystem, supported by strong governmental backing. Countries like France and Germany have national AI strategies that focus on research, talent, and ethics. Given Europe's emphasis on data protection, such as GDPR, executives should align their AI strategies with European data protection standards to ensure compliance and build trust[3].

Emerging Markets in AI

Emerging nations are making significant contributions to the AI domain. For example, Singapore's "Smart Nation" initiative demonstrates how smaller countries can leverage AI to address local challenges and gain global recognition. Similarly, countries like India and Brazil are investing in AI education and infrastructure with the aim of becoming key players in the near future. For executives, these emerging markets offer unique opportunities. Consider investing in AI education and infrastructure partnerships in these countries to tap into local talent and innovation.

Regulatory Environment

Regulations concerning data privacy and AI ethics differ globally. Aditya Mohan emphasized the importance of international standards for interoperability. He mentioned, "For interoperability, it is best that our standards are the same as standards elsewhere... we contribute as a member nation to ISO standards and to European standards through ISO and CEN." Executives must understand that these data privacy laws are setting global standards and adapt their strategies accordingly[4].

For executives, understanding these global standards is crucial. It's advisable to conduct a comprehensive audit of your organisation's AI capabilities and needs in the context of these global regulations. This will help you identify gaps and opportunities for leveraging AI effectively across different geographies. Furthermore, consider developing or adopting an ethical AI framework that aligns with both global standards and local regulations. This approach will not only safeguard your organisation against legal repercussions but also build trust among consumers and stakeholders.

Market Dynamics

Local market conditions, including customer behaviour, competition level, technological infrastructure, and economic health, are crucial factors in shaping AI strategies. These conditions can offer simple yet effective solutions for AI deployment.

For executives, understanding local market dynamics is essential for successful AI implementation. Consider forming strategic partnerships with local businesses or consultancies to gain deeper insights into customer behaviour and market trends. Additionally, invest in robust cloud solutions and edge computing to ensure seamless AI deployment that aligns with the technological infrastructure of the region. This will enable your organisation to adapt its AI strategies to local market conditions effectively.

Cultural Nuances

Cultural factors, such as language, societal norms, and general attitudes towards technology, play a significant role in AI adoption. These elements can either accelerate or impede the integration of AI solutions. For instance, some cultures may have a higher level of trust in technology, while in others, traditional methods may be more prevalent.

For executives, understanding these cultural nuances is vital for the successful deployment of AI solutions. Investing in cultural sensitivity training programmes can educate your team on the diverse attitudes towards technology in different regions. Furthermore, consider involving cultural experts in the design and implementation phases of AI solutions to ensure they are culturally appropriate and effective. This approach will not only enhance the user experience but also contribute to the successful and ethical deployment of AI.

Technological Infrastructure

The success of AI deployment is closely tied to the technological infrastructure of a given region. Factors such as internet accessibility, prevalence of digital devices, and the maturity of the local tech scene are key determinants. Without a robust infrastructure, even the most advanced AI algorithms can struggle to deliver their full potential.

For executives, it's crucial to assess the technological readiness of the region where you plan to deploy AI solutions. Conduct a thorough infrastructure audit to identify any limitations that could impact the performance or scalability of your AI initiatives. Based on this audit, consider investing in infrastructure improvements or opt for cloud-based AI solutions that are less dependent on local technological capabilities. This proactive approach will ensure that your AI deployment is both effective and resilient, irrespective of local infrastructure challenges.

Challenges in Achieving AI Leadership

Navigating to a leading position in AI presents challenges, notably in safeguarding user privacy across international borders. For executives, proactive data governance is key. Develop a strategy that aligns with global data protection laws to mitigate risks and build trust. This will be crucial for establishing leadership in the AI sector.

Strategies for Fostering AI Development

Promoting AI development requires a multifaceted approach, with actionable insights being paramount. For executives, being prepared to act on these insights is crucial. Consider establishing a dedicated AI insights team to continuously monitor, evaluate, and act upon new data and trends. This will enable agile decision-making and successful AI deployment.

Author's Insights

In the ever-changing world of AI on a global scale, achieving success goes beyond technical skills. It demands leaders who can expertly handle the mix of technology, international rules, and cultural differences. This chapter is designed to provide you with the key strategies and insights you need to become one of these skilled leaders. As Aditya Mohan of NSAI emphasized, it's crucial to take a broad, globally aware approach when crafting your AI strategy.

Ensuring Strategic Competitiveness in AI

In a rapidly evolving field like AI, the key to maintaining a competitive edge lies not just in technological innovation but also in global alignment. An emphasis on international standards serves as a timely reminder. By adhering to these global benchmarks, organisations can ensure they are not just competitive but also compliant, thereby reducing the risk of regulatory backlash.

The Future of the Global AI Landscape

Actionable insights play a pivotal role in staying ahead amidst evolving trends and technological changes. Aditya highlights the swift progress in generative AI and its potential implications for businesses. Staying informed about such technological leaps can provide companies with a competitive edge.

Recommendations for Executives

1. Global AI Audit: Conduct a comprehensive audit of your organisation's AI capabilities and needs in the context of global market dynamics and regulations. Aditya stresses the role of international standards, suggesting that your audit should also assess compliance with these standards.

2. Cultural Sensitivity Training: Invest in training programmes that educate your team on the cultural nuances affecting AI adoption in different regions. Understanding local attitudes towards technology can be a game-changer in successfully deploying AI solutions.

3. Ethical AI Framework: Develop or adopt an ethical AI framework that aligns with global standards and local regulations. Aditya mentions the EU AI Act's harm-based approach, which could serve as a guideline for your ethical framework.

Conclusion

The ever-changing global AI landscape presents a unique set of challenges and opportunities. Aditya Mohan's insights serve as a valuable guidepost, highlighting the importance of a balanced approach that marries technological innovation with ethical and regulatory considerations. As we move forward, the ability to act on actionable insights and implement straightforward solutions will be the cornerstone of achieving exceptional results. In the forthcoming chapter, we will explore the future trends and technologies that are set to redefine the business landscape.

Footnotes

1. The Global AI Index
   https://www.tortoisemedia.com/intelligence/global-ai/

2. "High Tech Industry in China"
   https://www.msadvisory.com/high-tech-industry-in-china/#:~:text=With%20companies%20like%20Alibaba%2C%20Tencent,and%20other%20cutting%2Dedge%20technologies

3. " German promises huge boost in artificial intelligence research funding and European coordination "
   https://sciencebusiness.net/news/ai/germany-promises-huge-boost-artificial-intelligence-research-funding-and-european

4. " France positions itself to become Europe's AI hub "
   https://aimagazine.com/articles/france-positions-itself-to-become-europes-ai-hub

5. " National AI Strategy "
   https://www.smartnation.gov.sg/files/publications/national-ai-strategy.pdf

6. E112 Aditya Mohan NSAI https://aiireland.ie/2023/09/21/e112-aditya-mohan-senior-scientific-officer-at-the-national-standards-authority-of-ireland/

25. Chapter 25:

Exploring Emerging AI Trends and Technologies: Navigating the Future of Business

Key Takeaways

1. Edge Computing Revolution: The rise of edge computing is transforming data processing, emphasizing security, and enabling real-time decision-making.

2. Emphasizing Security: By processing data locally, edge computing can offer enhanced security measures, as data doesn't have to travel over a network to a centralized data centre.

3. Enabling Real-Time Decision-Making: The reduced latency in data processing enables quicker decision-making, which is crucial in applications like autonomous vehicles and industrial automation.

Introduction

In the preceding chapter, we delved into AI's transformative impact on global business.

Now, let's turn our attention to the emerging trends that will shape the future, including edge computing, quantum computing, and AI's role in climate change. As we approach 2024, the rapid evolution of AI continues to influence various sectors, presenting both opportunities and challenges

Top Trends in Edge Computing

25..1. Prioritising Security and Privacy

Edge Computing, in simple terms, is the practice of processing data closer to where it's generated, rather than sending it to a centralized data center. Businesses face significant risks from data breaches. The focus on edge computing solutions with robust security features is growing, aligning with broader AI trends that address trust and bias.

25..2. The Importance of Edge-to-Cloud Interoperability

The synergy between edge and cloud computing is vital. Achieving seamless interoperability is essential for efficient data processing and real-time decision-making

25..3. The Role of Edge AI and Machine Learning

Edge AI and machine learning are reshaping the business landscape. These technologies enable instant data processing and decision-making at the source, eliminating the need to transmit data to a central cloud. For example, in an industrial setting, sensors equipped with edge AI can swiftly identify and report issues, enabling rapid corrective actions that reduce downtime and costs. Similarly, retail stores can use edge AI to analyze real-time customer behavior, offering tailored promotions that boost sales.

25..4. The Impact of 5G Adoption

5G is the next generation of mobile network technology, which offers super-fast internet speeds and very low delays in data transmission. It enables quick and reliable communication between devices.

The arrival of 5G technology is set to greatly enhance the capabilities of edge computing. 5G is known for its high-speed data transfer and minimal delays, making communication faster and more dependable. To illustrate, if you run a drone delivery service, 5G allows for nearly instant data transmission and reception for these drones. This leads to improved navigation and faster deliveries. In healthcare scenarios like remote surgical procedures, the speed provided by 5G reduces delays, making surgeries safer and more effective. In essence, 5G boosts the benefits of edge computing by speeding up data transfer and enabling real-time decision-making, making your business more agile and efficient.

25..5. The Emergence of Edge-as-a-Service (EaaS)

Edge-as-a-Service for Scalable Business Operations: Edge-as-a-Service (EaaS) enables organisations to utilise edge computing capabilities without incurring substantial initial costs. By opting for a subscription-based model, businesses gain access to the requisite edge computing power. This democratises the adoption of edge computing for enterprises of all sizes.

For example, consider a chain of coffee shops aiming to offer personalised promotions. Utilising EaaS, sensors and cameras can be effortlessly deployed across various locations. These edge computing-enabled devices can identify returning customers and promptly send tailored offers to their smartphones, thereby enhancing both sales and customer loyalty, all without a hefty investment in technology. In summary, EaaS renders edge computing both accessible and cost-efficient, empowering businesses to be agile and responsive.

25..6. Quantum Computing

As we transition into quantum computing, researchers are focusing on creating stable and reliable qubits, and shifting away from noise. Quantum computing is expected to continue its development through optimisation, machine learning, and cryptography, opening up new horizons in various fields.

25..7. Autonomous Vehicles

The technology behind self-driving cars is advancing, thanks in part to edge computing. Companies like Altos Radar are pioneering new sensor technologies, making autonomous vehicles more reliable and affordable[1].

25..8. The Metaverse

The metaverse offers a new frontier for AI applications. AI facilitates extended reality (XR) content creation, providing businesses with unique avenues for brand interaction and product discovery.

25..9. AI and Climate Change Mitigation

AI is emerging as a crucial tool in climate change mitigation, offering innovative solutions in disaster prediction, renewable energy, and more.

Author's Insights: Navigating the Future Through Emerging AI Trends

In a 2021 podcast interview with David Moloney, Chief Scientist at Ubotica Technologies, we delved into the groundbreaking applications of AI in edge computing, including its potential to revolutionise space exploration[2]. Ubotica is pioneering the use of AI to process data directly on spacecraft, thereby enhancing both data transmission efficiency and enabling real-time decision-making in space.

This is not merely a technological marvel; it's a signpost for the future of business. The implications are vast, extending beyond aerospace to industries that rely on satellite data, such as agriculture and logistics. As we navigate towards 2024 and beyond, these advancements in AI and edge computing are set to redefine how businesses operate, offering them a competitive edge—quite literally.

But the impact of emerging AI trends isn't confined to the cosmos. On a more terrestrial note, consider the use of AI-enabled wearable cameras at business conferences. These devices can instantly identify and provide background information on individuals, transforming the dynamics of business networking. Such innovations are not just 'cool gadgets'; they are powerful business tools that can significantly influence outcomes in real-time interactions[2].

These examples serve to underline a critical insight: Emerging AI trends and technologies are not just buzzwords or theoretical concepts. They are practical, actionable tools that are already shaping the future of business. As we explore these emerging trends, it becomes increasingly clear that business leaders must not only keep pace with these advancements but also strategically integrate them into their business models for future success.

Recommendations:

1. Invest in Edge Computing Capabilities: Given its rising importance, businesses should consider investing in edge computing solutions.

2. Quantum Computing Preparedness: Businesses should start preparing for the quantum computing revolution by discussing quantum-safe security protocols with their IT departments.

3. Sustainability as a Business Strategy: Sustainability as a Business Strategy: AI-driven sustainability measures should be integrated into long-term business strategies.

Conclusion

AI continues to be a domain of exponential growth and opportunity. By staying abreast of these trends and adapting accordingly, we can unlock AI's full potential, benefiting both businesses and society at large. In the forthcoming chapter, titled "Embracing AI: A Strategic Blueprint for Tomorrow's Leadership," we will offer practical guidance on how to harness the full capabilities of AI for future success.

Footnotes

1. Techcrunch Rita Liao August 14, 2023
   https://techcrunch.com/2023/08/14/altos-challenges-lidars-dominance-in-autonomous-driving-with-4d-image-radar/

2. E67 David Moloney AI Ireland Podcast Ubotica
   https://aiireland.ie/2021/09/16/e67-david-moloney-ubotica/#more-1349

26. Chapter 26:

Embracing AI: A Strategic Blueprint for Tomorrow's Leaders

Key Takeaways

1. AI is transforming how businesses operate, and leaders must strategically and ethically integrate it.

2. Collaboration with AI experts, continuous learning, and ethical implementation are essential for successful AI leadership.

3. The future of AI holds further advancements, making it vital for executives to stay updated and ensure their organizations are AI-ready.

Introduction

Expanding upon our previous examination of emerging AI trends and technologies in Chapter 25, this chapter delves deeper into the essential strategies that leaders must embrace in the era of AI. Artificial Intelligence (AI) isn't just another technological fad; it represents a fundamental transformation that is reshaping the very essence of business operations and innovation. The objective of this chapter is to equip future leaders with practical guidance on effectively and ethically integrating AI into their organizations.

Understanding AI

AI presents both unparalleled opportunities and ethical challenges. It is becoming an integral part of modern business, automating tasks and enhancing decision-making.

Real-World Uses of AI

Throughout this book, we've explored real-life case studies showcasing AI's transformative potential. AI's impact goes well beyond tech giants like Tesla and Amazon. It empowers small and medium-sized enterprises to enhance operations and improve customer experiences. For instance, AI is seamlessly integrated into our daily lives, from personalized music recommendations on Spotify[1] to optimizing coffee shop operations at Starbucks[2], and even ensuring your vehicle's safety and performance, as seen with Toyota's predictive maintenance algorithms[3].

Ethics and AI

Ethics and AI are inseparable. As AI becomes an integral part of our daily lives, ethical concerns such as algorithmic bias take center stage. Ensuring transparency, fairness, and accountability in AI systems is paramount and non-negotiable.

Data's Role in AI

As AI's reliance on data becomes increasingly evident, business executives must proactively shape their data strategies to harmonize with AI objectives while adhering to critical regulations such as GDPR. Embracing ethical data practices is essential, serving to foster trust and protect the organization's reputation. Simultaneously, executives should strategically embed AI across their business, capitalizing on AI-generated insights to enhance efficiency, drive innovation, and gain a competitive edge.

Navigating the AI Maturity Ladder

As a business executive, advancing through the AI Maturity Ladder involves key steps. Start with a thorough assessment of your current AI capabilities to pinpoint your position in the AI adoption spectrum. Set clear AI objectives aligned with your business strategy, focusing on areas where AI can enhance operations, customer experiences, or products/services. Invest in the right talent and resources, ensuring your organization has the skills needed for AI success. Develop a robust data strategy, emphasizing data quality, security, and governance. Prioritize ethical AI practices to build trust. Cultivate a culture of innovation, test AI solutions before scaling, and regularly monitor performance. Encourage cross-functional collaboration, and design AI initiatives for scalability. Stay updated on AI trends to make informed decisions and maintain competitiveness.

Collaboration: The Key to AI Innovation

Collaboration with AI experts and cross-functional teams is crucial for aligning AI initiatives with overall business strategy.

The Horizon of AI

Advancements in quantum computing and IoT promise a seamlessly interconnected world, requiring leaders to stay updated on emerging trends.

Managing Change in the AI Era

Leaders must address potential resistance within organisations by emphasising communication, training, and stakeholder engagement.

AI and Leadership

AI is not just a tool; it's a strategic ally that can guide informed decisions and ground-breaking solutions. Leaders must envision AI as a partner in their strategic planning, leveraging its capabilities to drive growth, efficiency, and innovation.

AI and Strategy

Integrating AI into business strategy is essential for maximizing its potential. This involves identifying key areas where AI can add value, setting clear goals, and measuring success. A well-defined AI strategy ensures alignment with overall business objectives and creates a roadmap for sustainable growth.

Metrics and KPIs: Evaluating AI Success

Regularly monitoring KPIs like accuracy, customer engagement, and cost savings is essential for optimising AI strategies.

AI and Talent

Investing in talent development ensures the organisation has the necessary skills to leverage AI effectively.

Customer Engagement Metrics

For customer-facing AI applications like chatbots or recommendation systems, metrics such as customer satisfaction scores, engagement rates, and click-through rates are essential.

Cost Savings

One of the primary goals of implementing AI is often to reduce operational costs. Tracking cost savings attributed to AI can provide a clear picture of ROI.

Time-to-Value

This KPI measures the time it takes for an AI initiative to start delivering measurable value. A shorter time-to-value often indicates a more successful project.

Ethical and Fairness Metrics

Given the importance of ethics in AI, it's crucial to have KPIs that measure the fairness and ethical implications of your AI models. This could involve auditing algorithms for bias or assessing data privacy measures.

By regularly monitoring these KPIs, leaders can make data-driven decisions to optimize AI strategies, ensuring alignment with overall business goals and achieving sustainable growth.

AI and Talent

Talent management is key to AI success. This includes recruiting skilled professionals, providing continuous learning opportunities, and fostering a collaborative environment. Investing in talent development ensures that the organization has the necessary skills to leverage AI effectively.

AI and Customers

AI is revolutionising customer interactions, enhancing engagement, and building loyalty.

Author's Insights

AI is not merely a technological advancement but a strategic imperative. Ethical considerations are integral to responsible AI deployment. Collaboration with experts and internal teams can accelerate the AI journey, making it a collective rather than a siloed effort.

Recommendations

1. Ethical AI Framework: Given the increasing role of AI in decision-making, it's crucial for leaders to establish an ethical AI framework within their organizations. This framework should outline guidelines for data privacy, algorithmic fairness, and accountability, ensuring that AI applications are transparent and ethical.

2. AI Talent Development: Talent is a critical factor in the successful deployment of AI. Leaders should invest in continuous learning programs focused on AI and data science. Partnering with academic institutions for specialised training can also be a strategic move to upskill the workforce.

3. Customer-Centric AI: As AI continues to redefine customer interactions, leaders should focus on leveraging AI to enhance customer experience. This could involve deploying AI-driven chatbots for customer service or using machine learning algorithms for personalized product recommendations. The goal is to use AI to create more meaningful and engaging customer experiences.

Actionable Steps for Leaders: Implementing AI in Your Organization

While understanding the theoretical and ethical aspects of AI is crucial, actionable insights are what truly empower leaders to integrate AI effectively.

Below are concrete steps that executives can take to make their organizations AI-ready.

Step 1: Conduct an AI Readiness Assessment

Before diving into AI implementation, assess your organization's readiness. Utilize tools like the AI Maturity Model to gauge where you stand and what gaps need to be filled.

Step 2: Establish an Ethical AI Framework

Create a set of guidelines that outline your organization's approach to data privacy, algorithmic fairness, and AI accountability. Make this framework accessible to all employees to ensure a unified, ethical approach to AI.

Step 3: Assemble a Cross-Functional AI Team

AI's impact spans multiple departments. Assemble a team comprising members from IT, data science, marketing, and operations. This diversity will provide a well-rounded perspective on AI implementation.

Step 4: Partner with AI Experts and Institutions

Consider forming partnerships with academic institutions, AI consultancies, or even your industry peers. These collaborations can offer fresh perspectives and specialized expertise that your in-house team might lack.

Step 5: Pilot AI Projects

Start with small-scale pilot projects to test the waters. Use these pilots to identify challenges, measure effectiveness, and gather employee feedback.

Step 6: Scale and Optimize

Once the pilot projects prove successful, begin scaling them across the organization. Continuously monitor performance metrics and make data-driven optimizations.

Step 7: Continuous Learning and Adaptation

The AI landscape is ever-changing. Make a commitment to continuous learning. Keep your team updated with the latest AI trends and technologies through regular training sessions and workshops.

Step 8: Customer-Centric AI Deployment

Always keep the customer in mind when deploying AI. Whether it's through personalized recommendations or efficient customer service bots, aim to enhance the customer experience at every touchpoint.

By following these actionable steps, leaders can not only adapt to the evolving AI landscape but also become pioneers in leveraging AI for business growth and ethical governance.

Conclusion

Navigating the AI landscape requires more than technological know-how; it demands strategic foresight, ethical responsibility, and a commitment to continuous learning. As leaders, you are uniquely positioned to steer your organizations through this evolving AI ecosystem, ensuring not just adaptability but also visionary leadership. The dawn of the AI era presents both challenges and unparalleled opportunities, making it an exciting frontier for those willing to embrace it. In the chapters to follow, we will continue to explore how you can not only adapt but excel in this transformative age.

Footnotes

1. " How Spotify uses Machine Learning "
https://www.projectpro.io/article/how-spotify-uses-machine-learning/687#:~:text=Spotify%20uses%20reinforcement%20learning%20to,fulfilling%20recommendations%20for%20the%20users.

2. " Starbucks and AI: A Deep Brew Program "
ttps://www.aiplusinfo.com/blog/ai-data-driven-starbucks-deep-brew/

3. " Toyota's Predictive Maintenance Program "
https://www.emsstrategies.com/dm050104article2.html

27. Chapter 27:

Conclusion and Final Thoughts: AI for Executives

Introduction

Artificial Intelligence (AI) is not merely a disruptor of traditional job roles; it's a catalyst for innovation and operational excellence. Drawing from our extensive research at AI Ireland and interviews with a myriad of organisations, we find that AI is not only spawning new roles such as data scientists and AI ethics officers but also revolutionising conventional roles in marketing, sales, and operations. The onus is on leaders to shepherd this transformation through judicious investments in technology and workforce retraining.

Transforming Work with AI

Throughout this book, we have delved into AI's transformative impact across various sectors, including healthcare, finance, and retail. We've examined its influence on marketing, sales, and customer service. With significant technological advancements in AI anticipated in the next 18 months, along with shifts in regulations and consumer behaviour, businesses must be agile. This involves redefining job roles and investing in continuous learning and retraining initiatives.

Ethical Considerations

The ethical deployment of AI is non-negotiable. Leaders should adopt a comprehensive framework that emphasises transparency, fairness, and accountability, thereby benefiting both the organisation and society at large.

Learning from Others

We have presented real-world case studies from diverse industries, underscoring the criticality of data quality, ethical governance, and cross-functional collaboration for successful AI implementation. These narratives serve as both cautionary tales and best practice guides.

Staying Ahead with AI

The AI landscape is in a state of constant flux. Staying abreast of the latest advancements is imperative. This can be achieved by attending AI-focused conferences, subscribing to industry journals, and actively participating in online AI communities.

A Call to Action for Leaders

The time to integrate AI into your business operations is now. AI offers unparalleled insights into customer behaviour and enables the delivery of personalised, automated services. Embark on your AI journey by initially assessing your organisation's AI readiness, subsequently forming a specialised AI team, and ultimately piloting small-scale AI projects.

Conclusion

AI is irrevocably altering the business milieu. As we gaze into the future, we see emerging trends in quantum computing and ethical AI governance. The role of leaders is not just to adapt but to wield AI judiciously in preparing for what lies ahead. The choices we make today will indelibly shape our organisations' future. Let us commit to being well-equipped to adapt and innovate.

28. Postscript from the Author

Mark Kelly's Pledge for AI Advancement

At AI Ireland, our mission is to guide businesses through the AI revolution.

We're convinced that with the right leadership, AI can lead to groundbreaking improvements. in our daily lives. But we're also aware of the hurdles it might bring.

That's why it's crucial to equip everyone with the necessary skills and knowledge for the AI era.

To back this mission, all profits from this book will be channelled into AI Ireland's projects that prioritize education and community support.

Appendix A. Glossary of Terms

Glossary of Key AI Terms

Resources for Further Reading and Learning

Directory of AI Service Providers in Ireland and Globally

Recommendations for AI Courses and Certifications

AI Ireland's Role in Promoting AI Adoption

Glossary of Key AI Terms

This section presents a comprehensive glossary of fundamental AI terminologies. The aim is to help readers decipher the complex language that often surrounds the AI landscape. Here, we provide clear, easy-to-understand definitions of a wide array of AI terms, each one written to help simplify rather than complicate the intricate world of AI.

Algorithm: In the context of computer science and AI, an algorithm is a set of step-by-step instructions or rules that a computer follows to solve a problem or achieve a specific goal. Algorithms are at the heart of all AI systems, providing the 'logic' or 'rules' that guide the AI's decision-making process.

Artificial Intelligence (AI): AI refers to the simulation of human intelligence processes by machines, particularly computer systems. This encompasses learning (the acquisition of information and rules for using the information), reasoning (using rules to reach approximate or definitive conclusions), and self-correction.

Deep Learning: Deep learning is a subfield of machine learning inspired by the structure and function of the human brain, specifically the interconnecting layers of neurons that make up the cerebral cortex. It uses artificial neural networks with multiple hidden layers, allowing computers to learn from large amounts of data.

Machine Learning (ML): Machine learning is a branch of AI that gives computers the ability to learn from and make decisions or predictions based on data. Machine learning algorithms learn from data iteratively and allow computers to find hidden insights without being explicitly programmed where to look.

Natural Language Processing (NLP): NLP is a subfield of AI focused on enabling computers to understand, interpret, and generate human language in a valuable way. This technology is behind voice-enabled AI like Siri, Alexa, and Google Assistant.

Neural Network: In AI, a neural network is a series of algorithms that attempts to identify underlying relationships in a set of data by mimicking the way the human brain works. It involves interconnected layers of nodes, akin to the vast network of neurons in a brain.

Reinforcement Learning: Reinforcement learning is a type of machine learning where an agent learns to behave in an environment, by performing certain actions and observing the results/rewards.

Supervised Learning: Supervised learning is a type of machine learning where an AI learns to make predictions or decisions based on a set of labelled examples (i.e., examples for which the correct output is known).

Unsupervised Learning: Unsupervised learning, by contrast, involves training an AI using a set of unlabelled examples. The AI must identify patterns and relationships in the data without any guidance.

Generative AI: Generative AI refers to the type of artificial intelligence that starts from a basic understanding of a problem space and creates new content within it, ranging from written text to images, music, and more. It is a type of AI technology that learns and understands the underlying patterns in data and can generate new, original pieces of content from scratch.

By understanding these key AI terms, readers will be better equipped to comprehend the technical aspects of AI and how it is used in the business landscape. This glossary is intended as a handy reference tool, providing the definitions needed to decode the complex language of AI and navigate the AI revolution effectively.

Appendix B. Further Sources of Information

Non-technical/introductory resources

In the ever-evolving field of AI, continuous learning is key. As such, this appendix provides a curated list of additional resources to support your ongoing journey of discovery in the realm of AI. These resources span across a variety of media to suit different learning preferences - from books for in-depth reading, to online courses and webinars for interactive learning, to podcasts for on-the-go insights, and research articles for up-to-date scientific findings.

Books

- **"Superintelligence"** by Nick Bostrom: This book poses critical questions about the future when machine intelligence surpasses human intelligence, analysing the potential impacts on civilization.

- **"Artificial Intelligence: A Modern Approach"** by Stuart Russell and Peter Norvig: Often used as a textbook in AI courses, this book provides a comprehensive introduction to the field of AI.

- **"Life 3.0: Being Human in the Age of Artificial Intelligence"** by Max Tegmark: This book explores a broad set of AI-related topics, including consciousness, computation, superintelligence, and the potential futures enabled by AI.

Online Courses

"**Introduction to Artificial Intelligence (AI)**" by IBM (Coursera): This course provides a gentle introduction to AI concepts, applications, and use cases. Ideal for those starting their AI journey.

"**Machine Learning" by Andrew Ng (Coursera):** Taught by one of the leading minds in AI, this course delves into machine learning techniques and their practical implementation.

"**Deep Learning Specialization" by deeplearning.ai (Coursera):** This specialization covers deep learning, its architecture, and its application to various real-world scenarios.

"**Large Language Models with Semantic Search by Andrew Ng-** Anyone who has basic familiarity with Python and wants to get a deeper understanding of key technical foundations of LLMs and learn to use semantic search.

Podcast

"The AI Ireland Podcast": This podcast explores the applications of AI in Ireland.

Webinars

"**AI for Business Leaders**" by OpenAI: This webinar series covers strategic considerations for business leaders interested in leveraging AI.

"**AI Ethics**" by Microsoft: This webinar discusses the ethical implications of AI and strategies to ensure responsible AI deployment.

Research Articles

"**Building Machines That Learn and Think Like People**" by Josh Tenenbaum et al: This research paper discusses recent progress in AI towards building machines that learn and think like humans.

"**The Malicious Use of Artificial Intelligence: Forecasting, Prevention, and Mitigation**" by Brundage et al: This paper explores the potential malicious uses of AI and proposes ways to prevent and mitigate these risks.

These resources offer a plethora of knowledge, insights, and perspectives that can significantly enrich your understanding of AI. It's important to remember that in the world of AI, the learning journey is ongoing as the field continues to evolve and expand at an unprecedented pace.

AI Ireland's Role in Promoting AI Adoption

AI Ireland is an instrumental organization in Ireland's journey towards being an AI-ready nation. Recognizing the transformative potential of AI, this organization has committed itself to accelerating AI adoption across the Irish economy and fostering a vibrant AI ecosystem in the country.

AI Ireland's Key Initiatives

AI Ireland has undertaken various initiatives designed to catalyse AI adoption and strengthen the AI ecosystem in Ireland. These initiatives span across three key areas: awareness, education, and collaboration.

Awareness: AI Ireland recognizes the importance of awareness in driving AI adoption. It conducts regular events, webinars, and conferences to keep businesses, policymakers, and the public informed about the latest AI developments and their implications. It also releases regular publications, showcasing AI success stories and exploring practical insights into AI implementation.

Education: AI Ireland has made significant efforts to improve AI literacy in the country. It has partnered with academic institutions and online learning platforms to develop AI courses that cater to various levels, from basic introductions to advanced, specialized topics. It has also set up training programs for executives, helping them understand how to leverage AI strategically and ethically in their organizations.

Collaboration: AI Ireland fosters collaboration between various stakeholders in the AI ecosystem, including businesses, academic institutions, research organizations, and government agencies. It has established an AI Innovation Hub, a platform where these stakeholders can collaborate on AI projects, share knowledge, and explore innovative AI solutions.

Partnerships and Collaborations

AI Ireland believes that partnerships and collaborations are key to accelerating AI adoption. It has therefore collaborated with various organizations, both local and international. Some of its key partners include the Irish government, major universities, and global tech companies. Through these partnerships, AI Ireland can pool resources, share expertise, and catalyse innovation in the AI field.

Supporting Businesses in their AI Journey

AI Ireland plays a pivotal role in supporting Irish businesses in their AI journey. It offers various services to help businesses, from start-ups to large corporations, leverage AI effectively.

Networking Opportunities: Through its events and platforms, AI Ireland offers businesses ample networking opportunities. These provide businesses with the chance to connect with other AI players, learn from their experiences, and explore potential collaborations.

AI Ireland's relentless efforts have positioned the country as an attractive destination for AI investment, and a hotbed of AI innovation. Through its initiatives, partnerships, and business support services, AI Ireland is playing a critical role in shaping an AI-ready future for Ireland.

Appendix C

Executive Checklist for Calculating ROI on AI Projects

1. Define Objectives
- Clearly state the primary goals of the AI project.
- Identify specific metrics that align with these objectives.

2. Initial Investment Assessment
- Calculate the total cost of AI technology acquisition.
- Factor in costs related to hiring or training AI specialists.
- Include any infrastructure or software upgrades required.

3. Operational Costs
- Account for ongoing maintenance and support costs.
- Factor in potential costs for periodic system upgrades.
- Include costs for continuous training and development.

4. Data Collection and Management
- Calculate costs associated with data acquisition, storage, and processing.
- Factor in expenses related to data security and compliance.

5. Revenue and Benefits Estimation
- Estimate the projected increase in sales or revenue due to AI implementation.
- Calculate savings from process efficiencies or automation.
- Quantify benefits from improved customer experience or retention.

6. Risk Assessment
- Identify potential risks or challenges in AI implementation.
- Estimate costs associated with mitigating these risks.

7. Intangible Benefits
- Consider benefits like brand enhancement or market positioning.
- Factor in potential long-term strategic advantages.

8. ROI Calculation
- Use the formula: ROI = (Net Profit from AI Project / Cost of AI Project) x 100
- Compare the calculated ROI with initial projections or industry benchmarks.

9. Continuous Monitoring
- Set up periodic reviews to monitor the actual ROI against projections.
- Adjust strategies based on evolving results and market conditions.

10. Feedback and Iteration
- Gather feedback from stakeholders on AI project outcomes.
- Use insights to refine future ROI calculations and AI strategies.

11. Documentation
- Maintain detailed records of all calculations, assumptions, and data sources.
- Ensure transparency in reporting to stakeholders.

12. Stakeholder Communication
- Regularly update stakeholders on ROI outcomes.
- Address any concerns or questions promptly.

By following this checklist, executives can ensure a comprehensive approach to calculating ROI, making informed decisions about AI investments, and communicating the value of these projects to stakeholders.

Checklist for Pinpointing AI Opportunities within Your Business

1. **Business Analysis**
- ❑ Identify key business goals and objectives.
- ❑ Analyse current business processes and identify areas for improvement.
- ❑ Recognize repetitive tasks that can be automated.

2. **Data Assessment**
- ❑ Evaluate the availability and quality of data within the organization.
- ❑ Identify large volumes of data that can be leveraged for valuable insights.
- ❑ Ensure data privacy and compliance with relevant regulations.

3. **Technology Readiness**
- ❑ Assess the existing IT infrastructure and its readiness for AI integration.
- ❑ Identify potential technology gaps and plan for necessary upgrades or acquisitions.

4. **Skillset Evaluation**
- ❑ Determine the technical skills available within the organization.
- ❑ Identify training needs or hiring requirements for AI expertise.

5. **Alignment with Business Goals**
- ❑ Develop strategies to align AI initiatives with overall business goals.
- ❑ Define clear, measurable objectives for AI projects.

6. Stakeholder Engagement
- ❏ Identify key stakeholders within the organization.
- ❏ Develop communication strategies to gain buy-in and build awareness.

7. Risk Assessment
- ❏ Identify potential challenges and risks in implementing AI.
- ❏ Develop mitigation strategies for identified risks.

8. Project Planning and Management
- ❏ Define a clear roadmap for AI implementation.
- ❏ Assemble a capable project team and establish a realistic timeline.
- ❏ Include flexibility in the plan to accommodate the iterative nature of AI development.

9. Monitoring and Evaluation
- ❏ Define success metrics that align with business goals.
- ❏ Implement robust monitoring mechanisms to track progress.
- ❏ Regularly evaluate the project against defined metrics to assess effectiveness.

10. Continuous Improvement
- ❏ Establish feedback loops for continuous learning and refinement.
- ❏ Regularly revisit and revise the AI strategy to ensure ongoing alignment with business objectives.
- ❏ By following this checklist, executives can systematically identify and harness AI opportunities that align with their business goals

and lead to meaningful improvements in efficiency and effectiveness.

Appendix C Continued

AI Checklist choosing an AI Vendor

In the appendix is a scoring system to weigh different factors when evaluating potential partners.

Scoring Criteria:

Excellent (5 points): Vendor fully meets the criteria.

Good (4 points): Vendor meets most aspects of the criteria.

Average (3 points): Vendor meets half of the criteria.

Poor (2 points): Vendor meets a few aspects of the criteria.

Unsatisfactory (1 point): Vendor does not meet the criteria.

1. Evaluation Factors:
- Technical Capabilities
- Depth of expertise in desired AI technologies.
- Proven track record of successful AI implementations.
- Scalability and flexibility of solutions.

2. Industry Experience
- Years of experience in your specific industry.
- Knowledge of industry-specific challenges and solutions.
- Client testimonials and case studies from the same industry.
- Ethical Commitment

3. Data privacy and security protocols.
- Ethical AI development and deployment practices.
- Transparency in algorithms and decision-making processes.

- ❏ Organizational Alignment

4. Cultural fit with your organization.
- ❏ Alignment with your organization's values and mission.
- ❏ Willingness to adapt to your organization's workflows and processes.
- ❏ Collaboration and Flexibility

5. Responsiveness to queries and feedback.
- ❏ Willingness to adapt solutions based on feedback.
- ❏ Quality of customer support and post-deployment services.
- ❏ Data Handling Practices
- ❏ Data storage and backup protocols.
- ❏ Data access controls and permissions.
- ❏ Compliance with data protection regulations.
- ❏ Delivery Track Record

6. On-time delivery of past projects.
- ❏ Quality of delivered solutions in past projects.
- ❏ Client satisfaction from previous engagements.
- ❏ Communication Style

7. Clarity and transparency in communication.
- ❏ Frequency of project updates and check-ins.
- ❏ Availability for meetings and discussions.
- ❏ Cost Considerations

8. Competitive pricing.
- ❏ Transparency in pricing (no hidden costs).
- ❏ Flexibility in payment terms.
- ❏ Future Scalability

9. Ability to support future growth and expansion.
- ❏ Continuous updates and improvements to solutions.
- ❏ Training and support for future integrations.

10. Future Scalability
- ❏ Ability to support future growth and expansion.
- ❏ Continuous updates and improvements to solutions.
- ❏ Training and support for future integrations.

Evaluation Process:

1. Vendor Shortlisting: Based on preliminary research, shortlist potential vendors.

2. Scoring: Use the checklist to score each vendor on every factor.

3. Total Score Calculation: Sum the scores for each vendor.

4. Vendor Comparison: Compare the total scores of all vendors.

5. Decision Making: Choose the vendor with the highest score or the one that aligns best with your organization's priorities.

Appendix C

AI Integration Checklist for Business Leaders

This checklist serves as a comprehensive guide for business leaders to navigate the complexities of AI integration across various dimensions.

I. Financial Investment

- [ ] **Budget Allocation:** Ensure sufficient budget is allocated for AI projects.

- [ ] **ROI Analysis**: Conduct a return-on-investment analysis for proposed AI initiatives.

II. Operational Adjustments

- [ ] **Infrastructure Assessment:** Evaluate existing IT infrastructure for AI compatibility.

- [ ] **Talent Acquisition:** Identify or hire personnel with AI expertise.

- [ ] **Training:** Implement training programs for staff to work alongside AI systems.

III. Legal Complexities

- [ ] **Data Privacy Compliance:** Ensure compliance with data protection laws (e.g., GDPR, CCPA).

- [ ] **Intellectual Property:** Secure IP rights for custom-developed AI algorithms.

- [ ] **Contracts and Agreements:** Review contracts with AI vendors for liability clauses.

IV. Risk Management

- [ ] **Risk Assessment:** Conduct a comprehensive risk assessment for AI projects.

- [ ] **Contingency Plans**: Develop contingency plans for AI system failures.

V. Ethical Considerations

- [ ] **Ethical Guidelines:** Establish ethical guidelines for AI usage.
- [ ] **Transparency:** Ensure algorithms can be explained and understood.
- [ ] **Bias Mitigation:** Implement measures to reduce algorithmic bias.

VI. Environmental Impact

- [ ] **Energy Efficiency**: Opt for energy-efficient AI models and hardware.
- [ ] **Sustainability Audit:** Conduct an environmental impact assessment for AI operations.

VII. Continuous Learning and Adaptation

- [ ] **Performance Metrics:** Establish KPIs to measure AI system performance.
- [ ] **Feedback Loops:** Create mechanisms for continuous feedback and improvement.
- [ ] **Ethical Audits:** Regularly review ethical implications and make necessary adjustments.

VIII. Special Consideration: Cybersecurity

- [ ] **Security Protocols:** Implement robust security measures for AI data storage and processing.
- [ ] **Incident Response Plan:** Develop a cybersecurity incident response plan specific to AI systems.

Index

A

ACI, -87
AGI, - 7
Alan Turing, - 8
Amazon, -76, 80, 104

B

Benefits of AI
Benefits of Generative AI
Boston Consulting Group, - 52

C

CarTrawler, - 22
Covid-19, -57, 59
CTO of Healthcare, -58
Cyber Inc, - 32
Coca-Cola
Constant Contact
Covid19

D

Dall-e
Deutsche Bank, - 12
Deloitte
Domino's Pizza-, 26

E

Edge AI, - 16

Edgecomputing

EdgeTier , -25

ESB, -88

EU, -75, 76, 77, 78

EY, -50

Exscientia

F

G

Gartner

GDPR, - 15, 62, 72, 87, 98, 105

General Electric, - 10

GE's Predix, - 10

Google, -53, 63, 76, 80, 84

Google's LYNA, - 10

Goldman Sachs

GPT, -92

H

I

IBM's Watson, - 10, 53, 63, 79, 88

IT-OT, - 37

INFANT

ISO

J
John McCarthy, - 8

K
Kieran McCorry, - 31
KPMG, - 30, 50, 51
KPIs, -84, 107

L
Lidan, -102

M
Machine Learning
Mazars
McKinsey
Microsoft, - 31, 63, 76, 84

N
Narrow AI, - 7
Nasa, -63
NSAI
Nutella, - 32
NVIDIA, - 12
North American Bancard

O
OpenAI
Oxford University

P
PMC, -65
PWC

Q
Quantum Computing, - 16

R
RiskLens
ROI, - 21, 51, 65, 79, 80, 84, 107
Russ Morton, - 38

S
Sephora
SMB´s, - 37, 38, 40
STATSports, -88
Stem, -94
Superintelligent AI, - 7
Stitchfix

T
Tesla, -81
Travel Webinar, - 22

U
Uber, -63
UV, -88

V
Volkswagen, - 32

W
Webio

X
XAI, -41, 42, 43

Y

Z
Zalando, -63

Printed in Poland
by Amazon Fulfillment
Poland Sp. z o.o., Wrocław